The Future of Internet Policy

All of the short essays in this volume look past the rhetoric of technological determinism and reliance on the natural logic of the market to consider the power of law and policy to steer new media in one direction or another. Many of the essays look backward through history or outward across national borders. They all look forward to how today's policies will shape the future of the internet and society.

A particular focus of interest for some of the contributors is on the revelations that followed Edward Snowden's mass disclosure of classified documents in 2013, which revealed the U.S. National Security Agency's systematic and longstanding program of monitoring global communications. Some chapters consider different countries' varying approaches to regulating the proliferation of online communication, while others assess the current state of digital technology. They all call for policy interventions to solve market failures.

Portions of this book were originally published as a special issue of *Critical Studies in Media Communication*, a journal of the National Communication Association.

Peter Decherney is Professor of English and Cinema Studies at the University of Pennsylvania, Philadelphia, USA, and the author of *Hollywood's Copyright Wars* (2012).

Victor Pickard is Assistant Professor of Communication at the University of Pennsylvania, Philadelphia, USA, and the author of *America's Battle for Media Democracy* (2014).

NCA Studies in Communication

The National Communication Association (NCA) advances Communication as the discipline that studies all forms, modes, media, and consequences of communication through humanistic, social scientific, and aesthetic inquiry.

NCA serves the scholars, teachers, and practitioners who are its members by enabling and supporting their professional interests in research and teaching. Dedicated to fostering and promoting free and ethical communication, NCA promotes the widespread appreciation of the importance of communication in public and private life, the application of competent communication to improve the quality of human life and relationships, and the use of knowledge about communication to solve human problems.

NCA publishes 11 academic journals that provide the latest research in the discipline and showcase diverse perspectives on a range of scholarly topics. These journals are:

- *Communication and Critical/Cultural Studies*
- *Communication Education*
- *Communication Monographs*
- *Communication Teacher*
- *Critical Studies in Media Communication*
- *First Amendment Studies*
- *Journal of International and Intercultural Communication*
- *Journal of Applied Communication Research*
- *Quarterly Journal of Speech*
- *Review of Communication*
- *Text and Performance Quarterly*

The *NCA Studies in Communication* book series contains special issues from these journals, edited by leading scholars. The main aim of publishing these special issues as a series of books is to allow a wider audience of scholars from across multiple disciplines to engage with the work of the National Communication Association.

Available book titles in the series:

Cultural Studies of Rights
Critical Articulations
Edited by John Nguyet Erni

The Future of Internet Policy
Edited by Peter Decherney and Victor Pickard

Race(ing) Intercultural Communication
Edited by Dreama Moon and Michelle Holling

The Future of Internet Policy

Edited by

Peter Decherney and Victor Pickard

LONDON AND NEW YORK

First published 2016
by Routledge

2 Park Square, Milton Park, Abingdon, Oxfordshire OX14 4RN
711 Third Avenue, New York, NY 10017

Routledge is an imprint of the Taylor & Francis Group, an informa business

First issued in paperback 2017

British Library Cataloguing in Publication Data
A catalogue record for this book is available from the British Library

ISBN 13: 978-1-138-85561-8 (hbk)
ISBN 13: 978-1-138-30545-8 (pbk)

Typeset in Times
by RefineCatch Limited, Bungay, Suffolk

Publisher's Note
The publisher accepts responsibility for any inconsistencies that may have arisen during the conversion of this book from journal articles to book chapters, namely the possible inclusion of journal terminology.

Disclaimer
Every effort has been made to contact copyright holders for their permission to reprint material in this book. The publishers would be grateful to hear from any copyright holder who is not here acknowledged and will undertake to rectify any errors or omissions in future editions of this book.

Contents

TABLE OF CONTENTS

Citation Information

The following chapters were originally published in *Critical Studies in Media Communication*, volume 31, issue 2 (June 2014). When citing this material, please use the original page numbering for each article, as follows:

Introduction
Introduction: Internet Policy Crises
Peter Decherney & Victor Pickard
Critical Studies in Media Communication, volume 31, issue 2 (June 2014) pp. 89–91

Chapter 3
Be Realistic, Demand the Impossible: Three Radically Democratic Internet Policies
Robert W. McChesney
Critical Studies in Media Communication, volume 31, issue 2 (June 2014) pp. 92–99

Chapter 4
Hyper-power and Private Monopoly: The Unholy Marriage of (Neo)corporatism and the Imperial Surveillance State
Chris Marsden
Critical Studies in Media Communication, volume 31, issue 2 (June 2014) pp. 100–108

Chapter 5
The Return of Ideology and the Future of Chinese Internet Policy
Guobin Yang
Critical Studies in Media Communication, volume 31, issue 2 (June 2014) pp. 109–113

Chapter 6
The US Digital Divide: A Call for a New Philosophy
Sharon Strover
Critical Studies in Media Communication, volume 31, issue 2 (June 2014) pp. 114–122

Chapter 7
Crypto War II
Sascha D. Meinrath & Sean Vitka
Critical Studies in Media Communication, volume 31, issue 2 (June 2014) pp. 123–128

The following chapter was originally published in *Critical Studies in Media Communication*, volume 31, issue 3 (August 2014). When citing this material, please use the original page numbering for each article, as follows:

The following chapter was originally published in *Critical Studies in Media Communication*, volume 30, issue 4 (October 2013). When citing this material, please use the original page numbering for each article, as follows:

Chapter 1

"The Air Belongs to the People": The Rise and Fall of a Postwar Radio Reform Movement
Victor Pickard
Critical Studies in Media Communication, volume 30, issue 4 (October 2013) pp. 307–326

The following chapter was originally published as an online article in *Critical Studies in Media Communication*, (January 2015). When citing this material, please use the original page numbering for each article, as follows:

Chapter 14

"What Is Wrong Cannot Be Made Right"? Why Has Media Reform Been Sidelined in the Debate Over "Social Justice" in Israel?
Amit Schejter & Noam Tirosh
Critical Studies in Media Communication, DOI: 10.1080/15295036.2014.998514

For any permission-related enquiries please visit:
http://www.tandfonline.com/page/help/permissions

Notes on Contributors

Peter Decherney is Professor of Cinema Studies and English at the University of Pennsylvania, Philadelphia, PA, USA.

The late **Greg Lastowka** was Professor of Law at Rutgers University, New Brunswick, NJ, USA, and Co-Director of the Rutgers Institute for Information Policy and Law.

Becky Lentz is Associate Professor of Communication in the Department of Art History and Communication Studies at McGill University, Montreal, Canada.

Chris Marsden is Professor of Media Law at the University of Sussex, Falmer, Brighton, UK.

Robert W. McChesney is Professor in the Department of Communication at the University of Illinois, Urbana-Champaign, IL, USA.

Sascha Meinrath is Director and Founder of X-Lab, a future-focused technology policy and innovation think tank.

Victor Pickard is Assistant Professor at the Annenberg School for Communication at the University of Pennsylvania, Philadelphia, PA, USA.

Amit Schejter is Associate Professor and Head in the Department of Communication Studies at Ben-Gurion University of the Negev, Beer Sheva, Israel and Co-Director of the Institute for Information Policy at Pennsylvania State University, Philadelphia, PA, USA.

Josh Shepperd is Assistant Professor in the Department of Media Studies at The Catholic University of America, Washington DC, USA, and National Research Director of the Radio Preservation Task Force of the Library of Congress.

Inger L. Stole is Associate Professor in the Department of Communication at the University of Illinois, Urbana-Champaign, IL, USA.

Sharon Strover is Professor in the Department of Radio-Television-Film in the College of Communication at the University of Texas, Austin, TX, USA.

Noam Tirosh is a PhD candidate in the Department of Communication Studies at Ben-Gurion University of the Negev, Beer Sheva, Israel.

Sean Vitka is Federal Policy Manager of the Sunlight Foundation, a Washington, DC. based nonpartisan nonprofit that advocates for open government globally and uses technology to make government more accountable to all.

Kevin Werbach is Assoicate Professor of Legal Studies and Business Ethics at the University of Pennsylvania, Philadelphia, PA, USA.

Guobin Yang is Associate Professor of Communication and Sociology at the University of Pennsylvania, Philadelphia, PA, USA.

Introduction: Internet Policy Crises

At the 1998 Society for Cinema Studies Annual Conference in San Diego, film historian Rick Altman presented what he called a "crisis historiography" model for explaining changes in film technology. (It later became a chapter in his book *Silent Film Sound*. [Altman, 2004]) Someone in the audience immediately popped up and asked why he called his theory a "crisis" model when it seemed to explain the typical development of the industry. "Because life," Altman answered, "is perpetual crisis." Altman may have explained why today we find ourselves in another crisis of internet policy, and why that crisis is not going to abate anytime soon. We live, it seems, in an age of perpetual internet policy crises. Contentious policy debates over antitrust, media ownership, network neutrality, the Digital Millenium Copyright Act, censorship, privacy, the open internet, open access, retransmission fees, and spectrum management dominate newspaper headlines. It is now widely recognized that these once obscure policy issues will have a dramatic impact on the development of entertainment, news, and communication. In both the popular press and academic literature, we regularly read about how new policies will bring about the end of the internet as we know it or open up a new world just around the corner. The crisis rhetoric, as Altman suggests, may just be overstating the mundane fact that things change. But all signs suggest that internet policy, inherently contentious, will remain vitally important for the foreseeable future.

For this special issue of *Critical Studies in Media Communication*, we asked scholars who have been thinking about these issues for a long time to comment on the future of internet policy. The essays we received suggest a maturing field in which authors took account of the long history of media policy to evaluate the current state of the internet and project future directions. All of the short essays in this volume look past the rhetoric of technological determinism and reliance on the natural logic of the market to consider the power of law and policy to steer new media in one direction or another. Many of the essays look backward through history or outwards across national borders. They all look forward to the way today's policies will shape the future of the internet and society.

Several of the essays in this issue take up the revelations that followed Edward Snowden's mass disclosure of classified documents in 2013, which revealed the U.S. National Security Agency's systematic and longstanding program of monitoring global communications. Chris Marsden's historical take shows that mass surveillance and information control has long been a constitutive element of communication technologies, stretching back at least to the introduction of transatlantic telegraph cables. State surveillance, Marsden reminds us, "existed before, and we should learn from the past." Inger Stole similarly admonishes us for being shocked by the Snowden revelations, but she points to a different history than the one Marsden outlines. Stole suggests that mass surveillance began with the hungry machine of commercial advertising, which runs on consumer data. Data has driven advertising since the early 20th century, and with the big data of the internet come even more sweeping surveillance practices by both corporations and governments. Sascha Meinrath and Sean Vitka's essay focuses on some of the troubling implications arising from the Snowden revelations. For example, as widespread surveillance is increasingly exposed, internet users are turning to encrypted forms of communication while government and commercial interests are trying to stop them. While Marsden and Stole would remind us that encryption has a long history going back to ancient forms of military communication, Meinrath and Vitka demonstrate just how much things have changed, even since the 1990s. Increasingly, all forms of commercial, governmental, and personal communication are online. And the struggle to both protect and surveil information is escalating at rapid speed, portending what Meinrath and Vitka call a new "crypto war."

Different countries are taking very different approaches to regulating the proliferation of online communication. In his contribution, Guobin Yang looks at online communication in China since Xi Jinping took over leadership of the country. Although it is still early in Xi's tenure, Yang argues that he has introduced a neo-Maoist approach to governance. Xi is engaged in a subtle struggle to control China's national imaginary and dream life, maintaining stability through the exercise of soft power. Yang draws from his expertise to decode the diplomatic messages of Chinese internet regulation. Peter Decherney, in his essay, shows that many countries are attempting to trade in some control over information in exchange for commercial and political rewards. Capitals of digital innovation like Israel and South Korea have adopted US-style fair use over the past decade, and many other countries are considering adopting fair use statutes in the hopes of stimulating Silicon Valley-like technological innovation and promoting democratic speech.

Essays by Victor Pickard, Sharon Strover, and Greg Lastowka assess the current state of digital technology, and they all call for policy interventions to solve market failures. Pickard sees a systemic market failure that has endangered journalism, reduced access to information, and impoverished public interest media policies in general. In addition to breaking up oligopolies via antitrust measures, he calls for the creation of alternative communication infrastructures like nonprofit news outlets and community owned broadband networks. Sharon Strover offers a comprehensive analysis of the growing digital divide and the long history of failed attempts to close it. The answer, she suggests, is simply the political will to see the problem eradicated. Lastowka focuses specifically on videogames, which he argues both tap into an essential element of society and offer prospects for solving many social problems. But the industry has given us entertainment without education, and policymakers need to step in where the market has led the technology astray.

Kevin Werbach, Robert McChesney, and Becky Lentz offer some concrete solutions. Werbach, who co-led Barack Obama's (FCC) transition team, thinks that the agency has the potential to play an important role in the future of the internet. If the FCC can successfully redefine the scope of its authority, it is the logical body to ensure an open and accessible web that serves the public interest. McChesney offers large scale policy interventions based on three assumptions: that internet service providers have formed what is effectively a cartel, that other internet firms have become monopolistic, and that journalism is a necessary element of a democratic society and therefore must be nurtured and subsidized by the government. And, finally, Lentz turns the tables, arguing that the future of internet regulation depends on educators developing and teaching media policy literacy. Control over today's internet crises depends on engaged and informed students, who will go on to shape tomorrow's policies.

Peter Decherney & Victor Pickard

Reference

Altman, R. (2004). *Silent film sound.* New York: Columbia University Press.

"The Air Belongs to the People": The Rise and Fall of a Postwar Radio Reform Movement

Victor Pickard

The postwar 1940s witnessed the beginnings of a full-fledged broadcast reform movement composed of labor activists, African Americans, disaffected intellectuals, Progressives, educators, and religious organizations. Although this reform movement would never realize the full sum of its parts before it was quelled by reactionary forces, it would succeed in registering significant victories as well as laying the necessary groundwork for future reform. The following analysis draws from archival materials and interviews to recover a largely forgotten moment in broadcast history, one that holds much contemporary relevance for current media reform efforts and media policy issues.

The vehemence with which segments of the U.S. public criticized 1940s radio is difficult to overstate. In its 1946 year-end review, the *New York Times* found "radio subjected to more obverse and insistent criticism than the industry had experienced in the whole of its previous twenty-five years" (Gould, 1946, p. 9). Another article claimed, "Criticism of radio is not new, but in 1946, as the industry enters its third decade richer, more powerful and more excruciatingly vulgar and meaningless than ever before, impatience has reached a higher peak of articulate disgust" (Young, 1946). A Harvard report on American media noted, "One need be no soft paternalist to believe that never in the history of the world have vulgarity and debilitation beat so insistently on the mind as they do now from screen, radio, and newsstand" (1945, p. 30). While there was significant agitation against media in general, the most pronounced activism focused on the airwaves, leading *Fortune Magazine* in 1947 to dub it the "revolt against radio."

Although articulated most forcefully among intellectuals and activists, evidence suggests that the depth and breadth of public unrest was more widespread than a few malcontents. Community radio "listening councils" sprang up to monitor local programming. Films and novels such as *The Hucksters* depicting sinister media moguls and advertising agents attracted significant audiences and press attention. Major newspapers and opinion journals across the country—particularly on the left, but also in mainstream trade journals such as *Tide* and *Variety,* popular magazines such as *Reader's Digest* and *Life,* and business journals such as *Fortune Magazine* and *Business Week*—railed against the state of American broadcasting.

Much postwar criticism centered on the Federal Communications Commission (FCC), the government agency founded by Congress in 1934 to regulate telecommunications and broadcasting, and increasingly a target of activist interventions and public outrage. Indeed, FCC files at this time were stuffed with listeners' complaints, indicating a pronounced anger toward radio. While social movements pushed from below, progressive policy proposals such as the FCC "Blue Book" and the Hutchins Commission's radio report emerged from elite circles (Pickard, 2010a, 2011a). Many believed the postwar changes sweeping American society also could lead to structural media reform.

Postwar America

The postwar period saw a moment of transition and "reconversion" in the U.S., and core social institutions came under increased scrutiny. New Deal liberalism had begun to falter with the rise of an anti-communist, conservative resurgence (Brinkley, 1995), but, despite this political shift to the right, a window of opportunity arose in the mid-to-late 1940s when structural reform still seemed possible. American society was not yet in thrall to reactionary politics, and many social movements, including those supporting labor and civil rights, continued to agitate for reform. The former saw massive strike waves in the mid-1940s (Lipsitz, 1994), and the latter saw a spike in momentum as African American veterans returned from war (Barlow, 1999). As these groups sought fairer representation on the air, their activism increasingly focused on radio as a vehicle for advancing specific issues, as well as a target for interventions to restructure the medium itself to become less hostile to activist messages (Fones-Wolf, 2006).

A three-pronged assault against commercial radio came from social movements, progressive policymakers, and average American listeners who were upset with their typical radio fare. In particular, widespread condemnation of radio's "excessive commercialism" galvanized a broad canvas of critical press coverage and irate letters sent to the FCC (Pickard, 2011b). The radio broadcasting industry already faced uncertainty given the impending competition from television combined with a steep decline in revenue and loss of lucrative wartime sponsors (*Time*, 1946). For a brief period, historical conditions seemed ripe for a structural overhaul. Although this contentious moment would help direct U.S. media's trajectory for the ensuing generations, this chapter in the history of American media reform has only rarely been mentioned in prior research and has yet to receive its due attention.

Previous Literature

Many historical accounts touch upon 1940s radio (for example, Barnouw, 1968; Sterling & Kittross, 1978; Brinson, 2004; Hilliard & Keith, 2010), but few address discontent regarding its commercialization. Horwitz (1997) situates these years as the second of three key media reform periods, occurring after questions of broadcasting ownership and control were decided in the 1930s, and before public broadcasting was established in the 1960s. Van Cuilenburg and McQuail (2003) see 1945 as the starting point for a new policy paradigm of "public service" media policy, while Sterling & Kittross (1978) depict it as the "Era of Great Change." Havig (1984) suggests that popular criticism posed as a great challenge to broadcasters as did technological and financial disruptions. However, few histories have specifically addressed the importance of social movements and their efforts towards media reform.

In fact, previous foundational literature has argued that people were generally happy with radio (Baughman, 1992) or that significant reform efforts had ended by the mid-1930s (McChesney, 1993). Baughman suggests that in the 1940s people were largely satisfied with radio and that "critics of radio's commercial, oligopolistic foundations were few and far between" (1992, p. 20). Lazarsfeld ends his classic 1946 study with the observation that people generally accepted radio's commercial nature. Other historians see less complacency toward radio, but conclude that the fundamental questions of ownership and control were largely settled by the mid-1930s (McChesney, 1993; Smulyan, 1994).

Although much was put to rest in the 1930s when a commercial, privatized system prevailed over public alternatives—as McChesney's work convincingly shows—crucial questions involving broadcasters' obligations to the public remained. More recent scholarship is beginning to provide a counter-narrative by uncovering evidence that many constituencies were unhappy with 1940s commercial radio and resistance was commonplace (Toro, 2000; Socolow, 2002; Newman, 2004; Fones-Wolf, 2006). Noting how this criticism differed from the 1930s, Newman asserts: "Instead of an intellectual elite attacking the commercial industry, a popular and widespread critique of the advertisers' control over the American system of broadcasting emerged in 1946–1947" (2004, p. 291). Other historians have explored the media interventions of specific groups, especially labor (Godfried, 1997; Fones-Wolf, 2006) and African Americans (Barlow, 1999; Savage, 1999). In her study on the labor movement's radio activism, Fones-Wolf (2006) argues that the Congress of Industrial Organizations' (CIO) attacks on the NAB fomented a larger movement based on a "loose media reform coalition" that was both "wide-ranging" and now "largely forgotten" (p. 126). Similarly, Toro (2000) observes that postwar "political struggles over program regulation reveal the continuous presence of social reform groups as participants in the FCC's broadcast policymaking."

Despite these revisionist trends, a thorough history of the 1940s broadcast reform movement does not yet exist. While Fones-Wolf's emphasis on labor's role within this media reform coalition provides the first clear glance at how this movement operated, scholars have yet to provide a comprehensive view of its breadth, depth, and composition. Likewise, Toro observes that although a few scholars have looked at how media reform groups impacted policy after 1965, most "have fallen short in their examination of the role of social reform groups at the [FCC] prior to the 1960s" (2000, p. 9). Which social movement groups were involved in media reform in the 1940s, and what were their objectives? The following analysis is a first step towards answering these questions and recovering a largely forgotten postwar media reform movement.

Theoretical Framework and Methods

This study uses a Gramscian theoretical framework (Gramsci, 1971), appraising the historical processes of simultaneous hegemonic blocs *and* currents of resistance as power arrangements constantly re-legitimate themselves. Such a conceptualization of history and power considers media policy as neither natural nor inevitable, but resulting instead from constant conflict and negotiation, with multiple, shifting terrains of struggle, particularly at the discursive level. The following analysis also draws from social movement theory, especially "movement framing" (McCammon et al., 2007). "Discursive opportunity structures," as formulated by Ferree, Gamson, Gerhards, and Rucht (2002), suggests that social movements often begin as intellectual critiques that are opportunistically exploited by grassroots social forces. Media policy discourses in the 1940s reflect a growing cultural critique that dialectically combined with the beginnings of a popular radio reform movement.

To make sense of these ever-shifting discursive realignments, this study relies on historical methods, including in-depth archival research of activist literature, memos, letters, and personal papers connected to individuals and groups that participated in 1940s broadcast reform activities. Close attention was given to the personal papers of FCC Commissioner Clifford Durr, whose range of contacts serve as a lens through which to glimpse the inner-workings of a postwar media reform movement. Additionally, phone interviews were conducted with two Durr confidantes and long-term media reform activists central to the 1940s movement: Everett Parker, a leader of various progressive religious broadcast groups, and the late Norman Corwin, a famous radio personality and radio division director for a major progressive activist group.

Out of this research, a general narrative emerges that traces the rise and fall of a postwar media reform movement. Based largely on FCC Commissioner Durr's correspondences and various activist literature, the following analysis examines the anatomy of this movement—its tensions, successes, and failures—by focusing on particular groups, campaigns, and strategies. Groups not discussed in depth that were involved in specific postwar media reform campaigns include the American Civil Liberties Union (ACLU), Jewish organizations, and women's groups (Proffitt, 2010).

Although disparate, the core reform groups' media criticism and activism were remarkably similar and often coalesced around common goals and ideals, including fairness in media representation, the creation of alternative media, and increased access to media production. More specifically, to varying degrees all of these groups engaged with the policymaking process in an attempt to remake the American broadcast system along more democratic lines. Given the last decade's surge in media reform activism, this history is particularly relevant to our contemporary moment.

Labor Holds the Line in Dark Times

Labor was arguably the first social movement to organize explicitly around media issues. Alongside other nonprofit organizations including churches and educational institutions, labor groups like the Chicago Federation of Labor were early owners and operators of AM stations (Godfried, 1997, p. 133). Yet by the mid-1940s, most of these nonprofits had been pushed off the air. Finding it increasingly difficult to gain airtime on commercial radio, the labor movement began contesting a rightward shift in the nation's news discourse, particularly its overt censoring of pro-labor views and voices. Labor historian Nathan Godfried, pointing to a 1943 Federated Press poll that found 92% of the press was anti-labor, notes that it was not surprising that "the mass media reflected business interests and values," especially with groups like the National Association of Manufacturers disseminating anti-labor propaganda messages as "briefs for broadcasters" (pp. 210–211). An example of censorship included zealously purging scripts for a Heywood Broun memorial broadcast of any mention that he founded the Newspaper Guild (Ernst, 1946, 142–145). The *NAB Code Manual* gave broadcasters ample cover for excluding labor, claiming "Discussion—or dramatization—of labor problems on the air is almost always of a controversial nature" (quoted in Ernst, p. 145).

Although industry would benefit from the 1947 Taft–Hartley Act's chilling effects, the mid-1940s still held bright spots for labor's organizing and media strategies (Fones-Wolf, 2006; Lipsitz, 1994). The CIO, unlike the more accommodationist AFL, used radio as a public relations vehicle for organizing as well as a weapon against anti-labor employers. Godfried notes that while the AFL hierarchy had "no grievance against" commercial radio, the CIO wanted to "meet propaganda with propaganda" (1997, pp. 210–211). The CIO's political action committee galvanized reformers with its *Radio handbook* (1944), which contained instructions for getting on the air and promoting "freedom to listen."

In the pamphlet's preface, CIO president Philip Murray wrote that the Labor Movement believes "that the years immediately ahead are the most critical we have ever faced," and thus "the people" must be "kept alert and informed as to their political interests." "In this task," he stated, "radio will inevitably play a very important part (CIO, 1944, pp. 2–5). Murray concluded that labor leaders and all those interested in "freedom of the air" must know their rights so that "radio is used as intended, namely, to serve the best interest of the people." The people's right to the air was a recurring theme throughout the handbook. Seeing radio as an underutilized resource, the pamphlet stated that workers "have not taken full advantage of their *right* to use radio broadcasting." "Labor has a voice," the pamphlet stated, and "people have a right to hear it." Although radio stations and equipment belong to broadcasters, "the air over which the broadcasts are made does not belong to companies or corporations. *The air belongs to the people*" (CIO, 1944, p. 6 original emphases).

Variations of "The air belongs to the people" served as a common rallying cry for 1940s media reformers. For example, in the 1948 pamphlet "The radio listener's bill of rights" (written by *FCC Blue Book* author Charles Siepmann) the Anti-Defamation League emphasized, "The essential knowledge you must have—and spread—about radio is the fact that it is yours. *The wavelengths of the air belong to the people of America*" (p. 44). This slogan struck at the central absurdity of a commercial system monopolizing a crucial public resource only to exclude voices of wide swathes of the population. This heavily biased system struck many as inherently unjust, as illustrated by one listener's comments: "While I am not a member of any union, as a patriotic American I am greatly interested in all sides of a question" (Keator, 1947).

The *CIO Radio handbook* provided instructions for gaining radio time for a labor point of view via several discursive techniques, including "The straight talk," "The round table discussion," "The spot announcement," and "The dramatic radio play." The book encouraged activists to generate good publicity, advising them to "not hesitate to send out your announcements to consumer groups, cooperatives, women's organizations, fraternal and religious organizations." The book emphasized, "*The more all these community organizations know about you and your ideas on national and local problems, the better you will be able to cooperate with them in any problem requiring political action*" (p. 25). The handbook also provided advice about choosing optimal airtime (evenings, although difficult to attain), tips on making high-quality programs that were not "tight-laced" or "too dull," and sample scripts for announcements and dramatizations titled "Are you registered?" and "What is the PAC?" Suggested topics included: "Labor's war record," "Child care and school lunch programs," "G.I. Joe and CIO," "Why we are for FDR," "The need for farm-labor unity," "The negro in 1944," and "Women war workers" (p. 23).

The book recommended responses to denied airtime included asking for the station manager's refusal in writing, writing a response, and sending copies of all letters to the FCC Chairman. Noting "the tremendous influence" a letter of protest can have if sent to contest "labor-baiting or any other objectionable programs," the handbook also instructed readers to ask members "to report to your Radio Committee any programs or any statements over the radio which are unfair to labor, or tend to incite people against the Negro or the foreign-born, or sound pro-Nazi or pro-Axis, or in any other way are directed against the best interests of the people." In these cases, the radio committee should "write letters of protest to the station, the sponsor of the program, the commentator or speaker" (CIO, 1944, pp. 30–32). The book concluded by asking readers about difficulty in placing programs; if their station carried pro-labor programming; and if labor representatives served on their local NAB listening council (CIO, 1944, p. 47).

The CIO also helped form the National Citizens Political Action Committee to organize petition and letter-writing campaigns urging the FCC to ensure equal time for labor perspectives and to provide more quality programming. Even as they continued fighting for an AM radio presence, many labor groups saw FM as a new theater of contestation, leading to an aggressive campaign for FM licenses to establish a foothold in radio markets across the nation. Unions attempted to gain airtime to offset propaganda and misrepresentation in the daily press and especially newspaper-owned stations (Ernst, 1946, p. 145). A major part of this struggle was challenging commercial stations' license-renewals for not upholding the public interest. The first of these campaigns was launched against WHKC, which had censored the UAW-CIO vice president's speech (Rosenberg, 1949).

Despite agreeing that demonstrable anti-labor bias ran counter to a station's public interest mandate, the FCC rejected the union's petition and renewed WHKC's license. The commission nonetheless agreed to hold hearings on the union's "petition to reconsider," which drew luminaries like the inveterate media industry attorney Louis Caldwell. Caldwell challenged the entire premise of the hearing as an attack on the First Amendment and the FCC's original mandate to not police programming. In response, the UAW began a long tradition of media reformers using media content analyses to marshal evidence disproving commercial radio's purported neutrality. Ultimately, the station agreed to stop censoring labor-friendly scripts and to air a diversity of viewpoints on issues important to labor groups. Moreover, the FCC's decision forced the NAB to amend its code's "no controversial issues" clause (Toro 2000).

In addition to establishing an important role for reform groups during regulatory debates, this episode set an important precedent for defining broadcasters' affirmative responsibilities to the public, helping set the stage for the later Fairness Doctrine (Simmons, 1978, p. 39). Stations across the country began to include labor voices, often in direct opposition to powerful anti-labor politicians. Broadcasters' policy shift drew praise from labor's sympathizers. An article by Corwin and Reitman (1945) noted that "Labor had waited a long time for this recognition." According to the article, it was inconceivable that organized labor, the second largest membership in the country after churches, was not allowed to pay for airtime, while employer associations were given millions of dollars' worth of free time to present their views. Supporters also noted that Labor had been forbidden to recruit members over the air, while employers could recruit employees and "anti-labor agitators" who were "permitted to air their biases daily" (p. 219).

Later that year, in a significant victory for the labor movement, the NAB formally discontinued its code. For a brief time, labor enjoyed greater parity on the air. The price of inclusion, however, was often to force more leftist groups off the air and to silence the radical edge of labor's critique of capitalism. These concessions arguably discouraged on-air labor groups from confronting postwar repression and racism (Razlogova, 2007). Nonetheless, the CIO's radio strategy was consistent with its larger social democratic vision emphasizing egalitarianism and expanded First Amendment freedoms. Although internal divisions undermined their effectiveness somewhat, unions often joined forces with African Americans, educators, religious groups, and intellectuals to mount campaigns against commercial radio's excesses.

African Americans' Radio Activism

African Americans had many reasons to work toward a more democratic and inclusive media system. They were

> especially astute to radio's unique power, reach, and influence, an awareness that emerged in the protests against *Amos 'n' Andy* and grew as the medium matured through the 1930s and 1940s. [Radio's] ability to present politically charged aural images repeatedly and simultaneously to millions of listeners moved what we now call "the politics of representation" into a whole new realm. Attempts to manage and influence those representations would have to become a part of ongoing strategies for African American political and economic advancement. (Savage, 1999, p. 11)

Contesting powerful commercial broadcasters would be an uphill but essential battle. African Americans also acutely understood how commercial media's structural biases—especially labor and economic relations—produced such demeaning imagery and fostered bigotry and disenfranchisement. A letter to FCC Commissioner Durr from a prominent member of the National Negro Congress stated the problem as being two-fold: "First, the widespread discrimination in the employment of Negroes in almost every job category; and second, the stereotyping of Negro characters over the air" (Cadden, 1947). Another letter from a returning African American veteran, disgusted by the radio fare he was subjected to and the "race hatred" it fostered, wrote: "It is too often the practice of vehicles of American propaganda such as . . . the radio to depict the American Negro as a buffoon, lazy, shiftless, superstitious, ignorant, loose and servile" (Tymous, 1946).

Economic concerns drove much of this criticism. During a discussion of the "Social Responsibility of Radio," organized by the Institute for Education by Radio, Lester Granger, a representative from the National Urban League, noted that his organization's "first concern" was the "equality of economic opportunities for Negro citizens" (Tyler & Dasher, 1946, p. 162). Radio had stymied economic progress by perpetuating "some of the stock characterizations and caricatures of the printed word, the stage, and the screen, thus advancing stereotypes and continuing racial misconception." Noting that depictions of African Americans had not changed for many years—exemplified by popular shows such as *Duffy's Tavern* and *Amos 'n' Andy*—Granger (Tyler & Dasher, 1946, p. 162) pointed out that a young person in 1946 "may not recognize the black-face minstrel caricature of by-gone days as radio's 'Rochester' of today." He also observed that African American bands were passed over for contracts given to white bands, primarily due to advertisers' influence. Finally, his greatest indictment against radio was its lack of job opportunities for African Americans:

> Outside of the entertainers in radio—the musicians, singers, actors, and comedians—there are scarcely two dozen colored men and women employed in

the radio industry, behind the scenes where the wheels of radio are turning. And there are thousands of jobs in an industry that provides 130 million people with almost continuous radio listening. And there are hundreds of job classifications— pages and pagettes, file clerks, messengers, stenographers, typists, cashiers, book- keepers, teletypists, research assistants, librarians, sound effects technicians, electricians; studio, maintenance, and recording engineers; artists, telephone operators, news analysts, announcers, scriptwriters, carpenters, firemen, private police—but almost no faces of my hue appear until...the janitors, the porters, the maids! (pp. 162–166)

In some cases, African Americans were hired temporarily as freelance voice coaches or programming consultants, but never as permanent staff (Rothenbuhler & McCourt, 2002, p. 373; Barlow, 1999). African American advertising also faced discrimination. One letter from Gainesville, Florida to the Southern Conference for Human Welfare complained that "although a substantial proportion of radio listeners and total business in the community is Negro, all radio stations in the community refuse to accept advertising by Negro businesses at any time, on more or less spurious grounds" (Dombrowski, 1947).

Increasingly, this blatant racism served as a rallying point for all progressive radio reformers. Reform groups called for removing on-air negative stereotypes and for hiring more African Americans. They encouraged communities to exercise their rights as listeners, scrutinize local radio, and not be afraid to call stations to complain when they failed to serve the public. Setting up "listening posts" to monitor broadcasts for balanced commentary, they coordinated with progressive allies in the FCC, especially Durr, who joined with labor and civil rights leaders to advocate for "listener's rights" (Toro, 2000; Fones-Wolf, 2006). The National Association for the Advancement of Colored People (NAACP), whose Radio Committee teamed up with other reform groups in the late 1940s, organized consumer boycotts and used the courts to pressure media outlets to improve their treatment of African Americans (Toro, 2000, pp. 52–54). Their tactics raised awareness of stereotypes and helped increase the number of African-American-oriented shows, many with black disc jockeys. Benefitting from African Americans' growing clout as a consumer group, these shows jumped from a handful in the late 1940s to over 200 by 1952. Although black-owned radio outlets were rare—unlike newspapers such as the *Chicago Defender* and the *Pittsburgh Courier*—legitimating African American programming was a significant accomplishment.

Despite these advances, the overall success for African American reform efforts was mixed. The practice of blacklisting and other red-baiting tactics ruined many of the most outspoken activists' careers and helped demobilize progressive groups. Those victimized during this period included some of the most accomplished African American artists and intellectuals such as Paul Robeson, Langston Hughes, and Canada Lee (Biondi, pp. 176–177). Robeson would never recover from having his career destroyed; Hughes was harassed by Senator McCarthy; Lee faced continued blacklisting and died in 1952 at the age of 45, shortly before he was to be questioned by the House Un-American Activities Committee (HUAC).

Progressive Dissident Intellectuals

Dissident intellectuals provided the media reform movement with another base of support. One exemplar, the People's Radio Foundation (PRF), was a NYC-based organization composed of left-wing and progressive groups mobilizing around media issues. Founded in October 1944 and composed of trade union leaders, labor activists, editors, publishers, writers, and artists, the PRF sought a "people's FM network" to air uncensored labor and progressive views. Its vision came out of discussions between the future PRF director, Joseph Brodsky, a prominent labor lawyer; Leslie Goldman, a labor editor; and Eugene Konecky, a former director of radio publicity, commercial, and program for an NBC affiliate station. Konecky had written *Daily Worker* and *Sunday Worker* articles about the potential of liberal and labor-owned FM stations, which reportedly drew hundreds of positive letters from around the country.

The PRF was stymied by a triad of powerful interests: state officials such as J. Edgar Hoover and HUAC; reactionaries such as ultra-conservative American Legion members; and industry representatives such as the Chamber of Commerce (Konecky, 1948, pp. 102–106). Despite formidable adversaries, the PRF's campaign for a broadcast license received considerable support: charter members included labor leaders from the New York Newspaper Guild, the National Maritime Union, and the American Communication Association. The new organization also included women's leagues, African American groups, and veterans associations as well as many leading intellectuals and artists, big-name backers such as Eugene O'Neil, Norman Corwin, and Charlie Chaplin. Following a 10-month campaign, the PRF sold $60,000 in preferred stock to approximately 400 individuals and organizations for the proposed station.

PRF programming plans included a show called *The Minorities are Major*, relying on various musical and dramatic formats to raise awareness about anti-Semitism and racism. To explore feminist history and experimental children's programs, they proposed a show called *Past, Present, and Future* (Fones-Wolf, 2006, pp. 140, 157–159). The PRF campaigned on an overtly pro-labor platform, with plans for shows like dramatizations of the history of labor; the story of the African Americans from 1619 to present day; forums with local high schools to discuss political questions; studies of American folk music; and experimental theater laboratories. Proposed programming took on political issues, including "frank criticisms of Congressional activity," and "case histories of social problems." The PRF promised only "informative advertising," for consumers union-endorsed products and vowed to bar "singing commercials" and "descriptive advertising." Permitted commercials would state "the facts about the product's function without spiraling off into a superlative exaggeration of that product's performance." Advertisers would be allowed no editorial influence; instead, the PRF's organizational model would be sustained by "the civic groups, unions, and the organizations represented among the stockholders" (Konecky, 1948, p. 108).

Pledging listener control over programming, PRF director Brodsky hoped to see community productions of "people's music, people's drama, people's dramatization" (Konecky, pp. 106–107). Prior to public FCC hearings, over 75 performers and technicians simulated a broadcast of several shows that the major networks had deemed too controversial—including one titled "Heil, Columbia!" whose scripts dealt with recent lynchings in Columbia, Tennessee. Another show addressed the specter of an atomic war. After the success of these performances, the PRF continued to rent out theaters to enlist local talent to perform shows, hold workshops, satirize commercial radio, and draw attention to local social problems. The PRF created a mobile company of actors and writers and a speakers' bureau of young people from unions and veterans groups to spread the PRF story to clubs and organizations throughout the city. Through a letter-writing campaign, they sent thousands of wires and handwritten notes urging the FCC to grant PRF a license (Konecky, 1948, pp. 108–109; Fones-Wolf, 2006, p. 158).

The PRF's decidedly left-wing orientation earned the ire of anti-communists who operated through various media. The pro-industry trade magazine *Broadcasting* repeatedly played up the PRF's communist links, including how Brodsky served as the Communist party's chief counsel for many years. Prior to the FCC hearing, the *New York Herald Telegram* ran a headline: "Reds in a drive for foothold in FM radio." Similarly, the *Chicago Journal of Commerce* saw the PRF's radio campaign as an attempt to please its "Masters in Moscow" (Fones-Wolf, 2006, p. 159). Despite this smear campaign—and the sudden appearance at the July 1946 hearing by The House Un-American Activities Committee (HUAC) investigators waving around FBI files on several PRF activists—hundreds of witnesses testified during the weeks-long hearings in favor of the PRF's requested broadcast license.

Months later, the FCC awarded licenses to five NYC applicants, but not the PRF. Following their rejection, the PRF disbanded and published a book titled *The American communications conspiracy* that explained the "aims of the foundation and of the FCC's decision which destroyed it." It insisted that any successful media reform movement must lead a "curb-the-monopolies drive" not reliant on the FCC's presumed progressive tendencies (Konecky, 1948, p. 33). "The strengthening of a people's anti-media movement is a better answer" (Konecky, 1948, p. 166), the book concluded. "Radio belongs to the people—it must be given back to them" (p. 42).

Despite its forcefulness, the book failed to impact radio-related policy debates and even drew criticism from some liberals, who were increasingly retreating from structural criticism (White, 1948, pp. 193–194). This was at least partly a result of intensifying red-baiting that rendered all unapologetically left-wing groups officially suspect. The PRF was included in the 1948 Attorney General's list of communist-classified organizations *(Federal Register 13*, March 20, 1948), and was targeted by reactionary groups such as the American Business Consultants, which was formed in 1947 by several former FBI agents and published *Counterattack*, a weekly "newsletter of facts to combat Communism." Alleging PRF connections became a standard method of red-baiting intellectuals (Cogley & Miller, 1971, p. 94; Barranger, 2004, pp. 228–229). *Counterattack*'s infamous 1950 report, *Red channels*, which smeared a number of artists and performers, listed many people associated with the PRF and similar reform initiatives, including Commissioner Durr.

The void left by the PRF's dissolution was in part filled by the Voice of Freedom (VOF) Committee, headed by Dorothy Parker and sponsored by an impressive cast of left-wing luminaries including Langston Hughes, Paul Robeson, and Orson Welles. In the spring of 1947 the VOF held a public rally that included recently fired broadcasters such as William Shirer, William Gailmor, and Frank Kingdon—victims of what many saw as a "purge" of liberal radio commentators. The rally staged an "imaginary broadcast" from an "underground" radio station to contest HUAC and other reactionary trends. The VOF would go on to organize nearly a thousand monitors and listening-post volunteers. These efforts were credited in forcing broadcasters such as the NYC station WOR to moderate their Cold War rhetoric (*Variety Magazine*, 1947; Konecky, 1947, p. 110; Fones-Wolf, 2006, pp. 125–126). The VOF also sought to cultivate relationships with progressive policy elites such as Commissioner Durr, who was invited to present an award to the United Electrical Radio and Machine Workers' Union for "its outstanding contribution to American Radio" through its weekly broadcasts of "Let the People Speak" (Parker, 1948).

Another leading left-wing intellectual group engaged with media-related issues was the Progressive Citizens of America (PCA), which formed after a merger in early 1947 of two other progressive groups (*Time*, 1947a). Henry Wallace gave a keynote address at their merger, with Paul Robeson listed as a vice-chairmen. By mid-1947, the PCA had 25,000 members, with chapters in 19 states (Adams, 1985, p. 11; *Time*, 1947b). At a meeting in New York Durr encouraged the PCA to write complaints to the FCC (Clark, 1947). The PCA kept in close contact with Durr via its radio division, directed by Norman Corwin. Corwin (2008) would later reminisce fondly about his experiences working with Durr, whom he said was a "broadminded commissioner," a "rare American," and an "inspiration," who had a "very benign role in the governing of radio," driven by the "common sense" of providing a "safety net for radio."

In April 1947, the PCA's radio division held a conference titled "Crisis in Radio," aimed at "dealing with the problem of radio today." Durr was asked to address "the legal and administrative basis for the public ownership of the air; rights, limitations, enforcement methods." Also invited was the NAACP's Oliver Harrington to discuss "the treatment of Negroes, Jews, Foreigners and Labor on the air" and to provide "an analysis of the objective of the stereotype." William Shirer, the purged liberal radio commentator, offered "a critique of the editorial role of the radio station as shown in its reporting of news" and discussed the challenges facing liberals on the radio. The Conference's statement stressed the FCC's importance in defending radio: "We reaffirm the principle that the air belongs to the people—to all the people." The FCC is the "proper defender of this heritage," and "must be adequately financed and staffed" and receive the "full support of the Congress" to "assure the re-appointment" of Commissioner Durr "whose actions and statements have consistently backed these [public interest] principles." Durr deserved continued support because "American radio does not now speak" for "labor unions, Americans who belong to racial and religious minorities, Young Americans who must be prepared for our future," and who together constitute a majority of people who are often under- or misrepresented by radio. The PCA also called for the "voices of liberal men and women" who were "deliberately and consciously shut off" to be restored to the airwaves (Anthony, 1947). Ultimately, however, progressives failed in establishing a major radio presence and much of their energies dissipated after 1948 when the Wallace campaign deflated and escalating red-baiting undermined many reform efforts.

Religious Groups

Media reformers in the 1940s included among their number various religious groups who mobilized to gain greater access to the air and to monitor representations of religious ideas and institutions. These Christian and Jewish groups would play an instrumental role in a number of policy battles; however, few were as active as the liberal Protestants led by Everett Parker, a mainstay in media reform efforts for over seven decades. Over the years, Parker played a key role in forging new coalitions and winning important victories, earning him the title "father of the citizen media reform movement" (Korn, 1991, p. 95). Through the mid-to-late 1940s he headed the Joint Religious Radio Committee (later renamed the Protestant Radio Commission). During the 1950s he worked closely with the former FCC chief economist Dallas Smythe in studying broadcasters' commitment to educational programming (Parker, Barry, & Smythe, 1955). Parker also would be instrumental in key civil rights victories around radio in the 1960s, particularly the landmark WLBT Supreme Court case. A campaign against the station WLBT's failure to serve the local African American community culminated in the Supreme Court determining that the FCC had to consider public interest complaints regarding license renewal even from groups not attempting to buy the station (Horwitz, 1997). Parker (2008) has noted that many of his media reform successes in the 1960s built upon earlier media reform efforts in the 1940s and 1950s.

In the 1940s Parker was a close ally to Durr, whom he befriended through frequent letter exchanges and meetings about radio reform. They collaborated around the FCC *Blue Book* as a vehicle to engage different communities and "teach minority groups how to protect their interests" in relation to radio. Noting that people in the 1940s were agitating not only against excessive advertising but also about programming quality, Parker recalled the strategic advantages of many different groups "working on the same issues at the same time in different places" (2008). Parker's testimony regarding the quality of local broadcasting during the 1948 Mayflower hearings led to revision of the FCC's no-editorials rule, eventually resulting in the FCC's Fairness Doctrine.

Sharing the assumption of many postwar media reformers, Parker saw in radio both democratic and fascist potential, a fate hinging on whether listeners engaged with the regulatory process (Parker, Inman, & Snyder, 1948). Parker (1946) expressed gratitude to Durr for having "taken an interest" in the work "to improve the quality of religious broadcasting over local stations." Parker hoped that "if our ministers and others who represent religion on the air can obtain an understanding of the problems and possibilities of radio" from people like Durr, "they will make a sincere effort to use radio effectively." Parker invited Durr to a workshop focused on "the question of how ministers of churches may lead in enlisting public-spirited business men to organize, erect, and operate FM stations solely in the public interest." Durr was to speak on "The American Ideal for the Broadcasting Station" followed by a discussion of "FM radio's advantages, costs, and potential services to the community." In general, Durr received much positive feedback from religious progressives for helping to prevent radio from becoming merely a profit-making tool.

Other religious groups joined the fray. A Methodist official wrote to Durr: "The evangelicals are beginning to come together for a serious approach to this vast field [of radio]." He added that "the upsurge of interest in religious life of the community from the standpoint of radio owes more to you than any other man in the Commission" (Tyler, 1946). Various Baptist groups contacted Durr to set up public service FM stations and promote other reform issues. However, the late 1940s saw a split in the religious broadcasting community between the liberal Protestants' radio commission led by Parker, and the Southern Baptist Convention, which sought to reserve radio spectrum to service rural communities via low-power stations. The Baptists sought to gain favor with the FCC over educators, while apparently lacking resolve in sticking with a nonprofit model. "The more I reflect on the radio picture with the coming of so many FM stations into operation," the Baptists' Radio Committee director wrote Durr, "the more I am convinced that the absolute key to any sort of success in broadcasting whether it be religious or otherwise, is programming." He was "convinced that we must move from the educational type station over to the commercial type" so they that we may "earn enough money to finance the best program of a varied type on the air." Fearing financial vulnerabilities, he notified all Baptist state radio committees to "swing from the educational type station over to the commercial type" (Lowe, 1946).

By the late 1940s, many advocates, including Durr, felt let down that the National Association of Educational Broadcasters (NAEB) and other educational groups were making little effort to defend their 20 allotted stations from the Baptists. In the end, media reformers compromised by pushing for set-asides for general noncommercial nonprofit stations. Although the PRF and ACLU supported this revised petition, its lack of support from nonprofits other than the Baptist Convention led the FCC to reject the proposal. Instead of allocating spectrum to general noncommercial use, the Commission limited special reservations to educational institutions, despite their sometimes-reluctant participation in broadcast reform efforts (Toro, 2000, pp. 70–75).

Educators

Educators comprised a core contingent within the 1940s media reform movement. Largely based at big land trust institutions in the Midwest, these reformers were adamant that a significant allotment of spectrum be set aside for educational purposes. By the mid-1940s, most noncommercial radio had been displaced by commercial broadcasters. One hundred twenty-eight educational institutions had launched broadcasting schedules in the 1920s, but only 35 remained by 1941 (Sterling & Kittross, 1978, 158), with a slight increase of 51 by 1945 (Ernst, 1946, p. 163). Although largely defeated in the 1930s, educators had regrouped to some extent in the 1940s to advocate for FM radio stations. They were aided by the U.S. Office of Education (Toro, 2000, p. 67) and the FCC, especially Durr, FCC staffer Edward Brecher, and Commissioner Walker's assistant, Walter Emery (Durr, 1945). Sometimes they coordinated to the extent of instructing schools on the precise wording of their official testimonies (Durr, 1974). Durr was an eager advocate, writing that there was "no subject" for which he had "a greater interest" than that of educational broadcasting" (1946). He saw existing university stations as potential seeds for a more democratic system. Expanding their presence in the new FM band would, Durr thought, force even commercial stations to raise their standards. "A few dozen—or preferably a hundred—good university stations operating on FM might not solve all of our problems [with commercialism], but they certainly would be a tremendous help" (1944a).

An important ally in both radio and educational radio campaigns was Morris Novik, the former director of WNYC (the municipal radio station connected to NYC mayor La Guardia). Helping to form the NAEB and serving as its director from 1941 to 1948, Novik was also the program director for the socialist-created New York station WEVD, and was the CIO's adviser on "radio propagandizing." He helped write, direct, produce, and distribute CIO unions' radio programming, including skits performed by steelworkers and dramatizations of labor news that were advertised via public demonstrations and handbills (Godfried, 1997, p. 197). Novik is also credited with coining the term "public broadcasting" and remained active into the 1980s.

Another active group of educators congregated at the University of Wisconsin and affiliated with radio station WHA, the "oldest station in America" and the first to launch an FM station in the state. In partnership with the U.S. Office of Education, this group had formed the FM Educational Radio Institute (ERI), which held annual two-week conferences to "serve persons concerned with the development of FM educational broadcasting in the various states" (FM ERI, 1945). The director described the conference's purpose to Durr as "concentrating on radio as a social force" (McCarty, 1945). Inspired by similar efforts in the 1930s, Durr advocated for 15% of new FM allocations to be reserved for educational radio. Acknowledging the "financial hurdle" for "nearly all colleges and universities whether supported by tuition or taxes," he confessed he did not "expect any great boom in educational broadcasting stations" to happen immediately. Yet, "if a few good ones get started," Durr predicted, "many others will follow along and in the course of five or six years there will be enough of them on the air to make a significant impression on our general broadcasting picture" (1974). Durr's plan was to ease in a handful of successful FM educational stations that would eventually overtake the commercial system.

Despite falling short of this goal, educators were more successful than other nonprofit groups, largely because the FCC, especially Durr, advocated aggressively on their behalf and requested special set-asides for educational radio. Durr urged colleges, nonprofit commercial stations, and other FM stations to embrace educational radio, because "the present interest among educators in FM is high." There was enough momentum, he thought, "to assure a good nucleus of university and college stations." Durr believed they could learn from the "experience of the AM educational stations which have managed to survive the trials and tribulations" (1944b). However, despite their general passion for educational radio, educators did not always unite behind the aggressive efforts that their FCC advocates and others felt were necessary (Gibson, 1977, p. xi). Harry Skornia (1945) confided to Durr, "I'm more convinced than ever that if education fails in the FM field it's education's own fault."

Conclusion

The major critiques driving a postwar broadcast reform movement can be summarized as the following: minority groups were neglected in representation and in hiring practices; programming avoided controversial subject matter; entertainment appealed to the lowest common denominator to maximize audience size and profits; advertisers' influence led radio to be solely concerned with selling unnecessary and trivial products; and, overall, radio programming failed to serve society's democratic needs. This criticism helped launch a nascent postwar media reform movement composed of labor, African Americans, disaffected intellectuals, political progressives, educators, and religious organizations. Although these groups often cohered around shared goals, they should not be seen as comprising one monolithic movement. However, their similar tactics included monitoring commercial broadcasting, intervening in broadcast policy debates, and advocating for their own representations, especially in the new realm of FM radio.

While Durr, Smythe, Siepmann, and other progressive policymakers hoped that an "aroused" public could rescue the stalled reform efforts in Washington, D.C., anti-communist hysteria undermined the last of the liberal New Dealers still in places of power and demobilized much of the nascent movement's media reform activism. By 1948, Siepmann's influence was mostly limited to academia and policy debates outside of the U.S., and policymakers such as Durr and Smythe had fled an increasingly hostile D.C. The FCC would be dogged by red-baiting and continue to exclude leftists well into the 1950s (Brinson, 2004). Moreover, many of the most prominent and aggressive activists in major social movements were removed from the political field by blacklists and sundry witch hunts. The Progressive Party lay in ruins after Henry Wallace's presidential defeat, and with the radical left purged from the ranks of the Labor and Civil Rights movements, many liberals were co-opted into corporatist, industry-friendly arrangements. Media criticism would persist, and lone progressive policymakers like Frieda Hennock would still serve at the FCC, but at least until the 1960s, despite significant exceptions, reform efforts rarely moved beyond the symbolic. The 1940s reform movement's defeat would leave in place a self-regulated commercial broadcasting system that would endure, with increasingly fewer public-interest safeguards, until the present day (Pickard, 2010b).

Quelled by red-baiting and a sudden rightward shift in the American political terrain, the postwar media reform movement would never realize the full sum of its parts. Coordination between various groups was often limited, and media reform a secondary goal. Yet despite its often inchoate nature, the movement did register some small but significant victories, and created a foundation for future reforms such as the Fairness Doctrine and public broadcasting. Overall, however, the movement failed in advancing its goals or enacting lasting structural changes. Contemporary media reformers have much to learn from their 1940s counterparts' successes and failures. Much has changed politically and technologically, but recovering past alternatives may inspire future reform efforts as today's media activists carry on where previous struggles were defeated.

References

Adams, D. (1985). *The American peace movements*. New Haven, CT: Advocate Press.

Anthony, S. (1947, April 11). *Correspondence from Susan Anthony to Clifford Durr* (Box 31, File 3) Clifford J. Durr Papers, Alabama Department of Archives and History, Montgomery.

Barlow, W. (1999). *Voice over: The making of black radio*. Philadelphia, PA: Temple University Press.

Barnouw, E. (1968). *The golden web: A history of broadcasting in the United States, vol. 2: 1933–1953*. New York, NY: Oxford University Press.

Barranger, M. (2004). *Margaret Webster: A life in theater*. Ann Arbor: University of Michigan Press.

Baughman, J. (1992). *The republic of mass culture*. Baltimore, MD: Johns Hopkins University Press.

Biondi, M. (2003). *To Stand and Fight: The Struggle for Civil Rights in Postwar New York City*. Cambridge, MA: Harvard University Press.

Brinkley, A. (1995). *End of reform: New deal liberalism in recession and War*. New York, NY: Vintage.

Brinson, S. (2004). *The red scare, politics, and the FCC, 1941–1960*. Westport, CT: Praeger.

Cadden, V. (1947, February 20). *Correspondence from Vivian Cadden to Clifford Durr* (Box 31, File 2). Clifford J. Durr papers, Alabama Department of Archives and History, Montgomery.

Clark, M. (1947, May 7). *Correspondence from Margaret Clark to Clifford Durr* (Box 59, General correspondence, 1947–1956), National Archives, University of Maryland.

CIO Political Action Committee. (1944). *Radio handbook*. Washington, DC.

Cogley, J., & Miller, M. (1971). *Blacklisting: Two key documents*. New York, NY: Ayer.

Corwin, E., & Reitman, A. (1945, February 12). "Is Radio Going Liberal?" *New Republic 112*, p. 7.

Corwin, N. (2008, December 11). Phone interview with the author.

Dombrowski, J. (1947, April 23). *Correspondence from James Dombrowski to Clifford Durr* (Box 31, File 3). Clifford J. Durr papers, Alabama Department of Archives and History, Montgomery.

Durr, C. (1944a, May 10). *Correspondence from Clifford Durr to Harlow Shapley* (Box 30, File 1). Clifford J. Durr papers, Alabama Department of Archives and History, Montgomery.

Durr, C. (1944b, September 6). *Correspondence from Clifford Durr to Robert Leigh* (Box 30, File 2). Clifford J. Durr papers, Alabama Department of Archives and History, Montgomery.

Durr, C. (1945, February 14). *Correspondence from Clifford Durr to H.B. McCarty* (Box 30, File 3). Clifford J. Durr papers, Alabama Department of Archives and History, Montgomery.

Durr, C. (1946, August 20). *Correspondence from Clifford Durr to George Jennings* (Box 30, File 7). Clifford J. Durr papers, Alabama Department of Archives and History, Montgomery.

Durr, C. (1974). Oral history interview, December 29, Interview B-0017. Southern Oral History Program Collection (#4007), University of North Carolina at Chapel Hill.

Ernst, M. (1946). *The first freedom*. New York, NY: Macmillan.

Ferree, M.M., Gamson, W., Gerhards, J., & Rucht, D. (2002). *Shaping aabortion discourse: Democracy and the public sphere in Germany and the United States*. Cambridge: Cambridge University Press.

Fones-Wolf, E. (2006). *Waves of opposition: Labor, business, and the struggle for democratic radio*. Urbana: University of Illinois Press.

FM ERI. (1945). Conference program, July 29–August 11. (Box 30, File 3). Clifford J. Durr papers, Alabama Department of Archives and History, Montgomery.

Fortune Magazine. (1947, March). The Revolt Against Radio, *35*(102), 101–103.

Gibson, G. (1977). *Public broadcasting: The role of the federal government, 1912–76*. New York, NY: Praeger Special Studies.

Godfried, N. (1997). *WCFL: Chicago's voice of labor, 1926–78*. Urbana: University of Illinois Press.

Gould, J. (1946, December 29). Backward glance, *New York Times*, p. 9.

Gramsci, A. (1971). *Selections from the prison notebooks*. New York, NY: International Publishers.

Harvard University. (1945). Committee on the objectives of a general education in a free society. In *General education in a free society*, Cambridge, MA: Harvard University Press.

Havig, A. (1984). Frederick Wakeman's the Hucksters and the postwar debate over commercial radio. *Journal of Broadcasting*, *29*, 2.

Horwitz, R. (1997). Broadcast reform revisited: Reverend Everett C. Parker and the "Standing" case. *The Communication Review*, *2*, 311–348.

Hilliard, R.L., & Keith, M.C. (2010). *The Broadcast Century and Beyond*. (5th ed.). Boston: Focal Press.

Keator, M. (1947, May 7). *Correspondence from Clifford Durr to Maude Keator* (Box 59, General Correspondence, 1947–1956). National Archives, University of Maryland.

Konecky, E. (1948). *The American communications conspiracy*. New York, NY: People's Radio Foundation.

Korn, G. (1991). Everett C. Parker and the Citizen Media Reform Movement: A phenomenological life history (Unpublished PhD dissertation). Southern Illinois University, Carbondale.

Lazarsfeld, P. (1946). *The People Look at Radio*. Chapel Hill: University of North Carolina Press.

Lipsitz, G. (1994). *Rainbow at midnight: Labor and culture in the 1940s*. Urbana: University of Illinois Press.

Lowe, S.F. (1946, September 23). *Correspondence from S.F. Lowe to Clifford Durr* (Box 30, File 8). Clifford J. Durr papers, Alabama Department of Archives and History, Montgomery.

McCammon, H., Muse, C.S., Newman, H.D. & Terrell, T. (2007). Movement framing and discursive opportunity structures: The political successes of the US women's jury movements. *American Sociological Review*, *72*, 725–749.

McCarty, H.B. (1945, January 30). *Correspondence from H.B. McCarty to Clifford Durr* (Box 30, File 3). Durr Papers.

McChesney, R. (1993). *Telecommunications, Mass Media & Democracy: The Battle for the Control of U.S. Broadcasting, 1928–1935*. New York: The Oxford University Press.

Newman, K. (2004). *Radio Active: Advertising and Consumer Activism, 1935–1947*. Berkeley: University of California Press.

Parker, D. (1948, June 3). *Correspondence from Dorothy Parker to Clifford Durr* (Box 31, File 9). Clifford J. Durr papers, Alabama Department of Archives and History, Montgomery.

Parker, E. (1946, January 22). *Correspondence from Everett Parker to Clifford Durr* (Box 30, File 5). Clifford J. Durr papers, Alabama Department of Archives and History, Montgomery.

Parker, E. (2008, December 23). Phone interview with the author.

Parker, E., Barry, D., & Smythe, D. (1955). *The television-radio audience and religion*. New York, NY: Harper & Brothers.

Parker, E., Inman, E., & Snyder, R. (1948). *Religious radio: What to do and how.* New York, NY: Harper.

Pickard, V. (2010a). "Whether the giants should be slain or persuaded to be good": Revisiting the Hutchins Commission and the role of media in a democratic society. *Critical Studies in Media Communication, 27*(4), 391–411.

Pickard, V. (2010b). Reopening the postwar settlement for US media: The origins and implications of the social contract between media, the state, and the polity. *Communication, Culture & Critique, 3,* 170–189.

Pickard, V. (2011a). The battle over the FCC blue book: Determining the role of broadcast media in a democratic society, 1945–1948. *Media, Culture & Society, 33*(2), 171–191.

Pickard, V. (2011b). The revolt against radio: Postwar media criticism and the struggle for broadcast reform. In J. Peck & I. Stole (Eds.), *A moment of danger: Critical studies in the history of US communication since 1945* (pp. 35–56). Milwaukee, WI: New Marquette University Press.

Proffitt, J. (2010). War, peace, and free radio: The Women's National Radio Committee's efforts to promote democracy, 1939–1946. *Journal of Radio & Audio Media, 17,* 2–17.

Razlogova, E. (2007). Review of waves of opposition: Labor and the struggle for democratic radio. *The Journal of American History, 94*(2), 608–609.

Rosenberg, H. (1949). Program content. A criterion of public interest in FCC licensing. *The Western Political Quarterly, 2*(3), 375–401.

Rothenbuhler, E., & McCourt, T. (2002). Radio redefines itself, 1947–1962. In M. Hilmes & J. Loviglio (Eds.), *Radio reader: Essays in the cultural history of radio.* New York, NY: Routledge.

Savage, B. (1999). *Broadcasting freedom: Radio, war, and the politics of race, 1938–1948.* Chapel Hill: University of North Carolina.

Schiller, D. (1996). *Theorizing communication: A history.* New York, NY: Oxford University Press.

Siepmann, C. (1948). *The radio listener's bill of rights: Democracy, radio, and you.* New York, NY: Anti-Defamation League of B'nai B'rith.

Simmons, S. (1978). *The fairness doctrine and the media.* Berkeley, CA: University of California Press.

Skornia, H. (1945, August 17). *Correspondence from H. Skornia to Clifford Durr* (Box 30, File 3). Clifford J. Durr papers, Alabama Department of Archives and History, Montgomery.

Smulyan, S. (1994). *Selling radio: The commercialization of American broadcasting, 1920–1934.* Washington, DC: Smithsonian Institution Press.

Socolow, M. (2002). Questioning Advertising's Influence over American Radio: The Blue Book Controversy of 1945–1947. *Journal of Radio Studies, 9,* 292–302.

Sterling, C.H, John, M., & Kittross, J.M. (1978). *Stay Tuned: A Concise History of American Broadcasting.* Belmont: Wadsworth.

Time. (1946, May 27). End of a Spree, pp. 92, 94.

Time. (1947a, January 6). Merger. Retrieved from http://www.time.com/time/magazine/article/0,9171,853003,00.html

Time. (1947b, July 7). Hot Time. Retrieved from http://www.time.com/time/magazine/article/0,9171,934613,00.html

Toro, A. (2000). Standing up for listener's rights: A history of public participation at the Federal Communications Commission (Unpublished PhD dissertation). University of California at Berkeley.

Tyler, I.K., & Dasher, N.D., Eds. (1946). "The Social Responsibility of Radio." *Education on the Air* (pp. 155–215). Ohio State University, Columbus: Institute For Education by Radio.

Tyler, R.Z. (1946, May 15). *Correspondence from R.Z. Tyler to Durr* (Box 30, File 6). Clifford J. Durr papers, Alabama Department of Archives and History, Montgomery.

Tymous, W. (1946, March 12). *Correspondence from William Tymous to Clifford Durr.* (Box 16–8, File 2–14). Dallas Smythe papers, Simon Fraser University, British Columbia.

Van Cuilenburg, J., & McQuail, D. (2003). Media policy shifts: Toward a new communications policy paradigm. *European Journal of Communication, 18*(2), 181–207.

Variety. (1947, March 5). Liberal gabbers go underground at VOF rally to blast speech curb, p. 30.

White, L. (1948). Review of "The American Communications Conspiracy." *Annals of the American Academy of Political and Social Science,* 193–194.

Young, V. (1946) The big noise of the Hucksters. *Arizona Quarterly,* 2, 5–12.

Infrastructure in the Air: The Office of Education and the Development of Public Broadcasting in the United States, 1934–1944

Josh Shepperd

This paper examines the origins of the institutional organization and advocacy strategies that later culminated in American public broadcasting. Previous to the Communications Act of 1934, which privatized American broadcasting, educational radio lacked standards for best practices and functioned in a decentralized and localized form. After the Act, the Office of Education (OOE) took interest in radio as a medium to expand federal initiatives related to educational "public forums," town-hall style meetings centered around community debate. Noting the lack of noncommercial channels in which to broadcast forums to a larger audience, the OOE began to collaborate with the National Association of Educational Broadcasters (NAEB) to lobby the FCC, while producing civic programming with commercial broadcasters. Instead of fighting the regulation, the OOE and NAEB founded an advocacy approach centered on creating an alternate broadcasting infrastructure as a way to address regulatory precedents. In this process, early forms of production, distribution, and infrastructure later associated with public broadcasting were devised out of a hybrid of commercial broadcasting aesthetics and federal educational bureaucracy. Contrary to the received view, discussion of the origins of American public broadcasting must be framed as advocacy to change the national system through strategies of research, collaboration, and governmental incorporation instead of resistance.

What happened to the media reform movement in the United States after the Communications Act of 1934? How did educational broadcasting rebound and ultimately evolve into national public broadcasting? This paper examines the strategic alliance that formed between local and national educators after the Act toward the creation of an educational broadcasting infrastructure. To this point, no research has examined how educational broadcasters built scaffolding for public broadcasting after the Communications Act, nor how the government first became interested in the possibility of a federal noncommercial broadcasting service. Contrary to the received view, the 1934 Act did not mark a defeat for educational broadcasters, but rather galvanized and increased its advocates. Between 1934 and World War II, educational broadcasting became associated with the Office of Education's program to defend democratic ideals from fascism through public education. This relationship not only centrally strengthened the effect of subsequent educational advocacy rhetoric, but also permanently tied educational public broadcasting practices to federal cultural initiatives.

As covered by McChesney (1993) and Slotten (2009), between 1921 and 1934, educators, largely at land-grant universities, believed that radio held capacities effective for swaying public judgment and promoting pedagogical initiatives that had originated in distance-learning programs and adult education courses (Ohio State Radio Institute Conference Proceedings, 1934). In contrast to the educators, NBC and CBS had invested dramatically in technological infrastructure, manufacturing, program development, and lobbying, and even developed a proposal for a national "clear-channel" broadcasting approach that could technically unite all listeners into a national broadcasting umbrella (Douglas, 1987; Slotten, 2000; Smulyan, 1994). The character of public airwaves—which owed a great debt to land-grant university physics experimentation between 1900 and 1921—was monolithically delegated to the networks with the Communications Act of 1934 (McChesney, 1993; Mitchell, 2005). Almost 100% of broadcasting frequencies had been commercialized, with few allocations left for educational broadcasters, though educators had never requested more than 25% (NAEB Bulletin, 1931) of possible wavelengths, with later proposals as low as 15% (NAEB Membership Ledgers, 1935–1937). However, the commercial sphere held little inherent interest in providing civic programming, and network administrators left advocates without access to experimental frequencies, regulatory support, or knowledge of their aesthetic research. While it has been argued that the Federal Radio Commission (FRC) was too closely affiliated with the commercial interests it was supposed to be regulating, many universities had not yet developed methods to translate progressive-minded concepts into formulized radio practices, and remained largely local and regionally based operations (for discussion of radio localism, see Kirkpatrick, 2006).

By the mid-1930s, only a few dozen school districts and universities held onto their licenses out of potentially thousands of available channels. However, the 1934 Act also engendered the unintended consequence of gaining the interest of the Office of Education (OOE), specifically John Studebaker, a former school superintendent with an interest in radio who had serendipitously been appointed as Commissioner of Education the same year. Studebaker became interested in radio as an extension of antifascist community-building tactics, which he called "public forums." Calling upon his progressive beliefs, administrative agenda, and educational experience, Studebaker was the first public official of his standing to lead the charge for a federally mandated public service broadcasting quotient. Directly proceeding the Act under the moniker The Federal Radio Education Committee (FREC), Studebaker's OOE helped to define the terms of debate surrounding the place of educational broadcasting as a national interest and unify previously decentralized educational broadcasting practitioners through the National Association for Educational Broadcasting (NAEB). In the process, the OOE introduced national pedagogical, curricular, and (for the first time) network production practices to local and regional educators so that they could craft standards for curricular content.

Through primary document research at broadcasting archives as well as federal, philanthropic, and educational collections, this paper argues that educational broadcasting evolved into public broadcasting in large part due to the structuring influence of the FREC upon noncommercial broadcasting organization. Further, this paper contributes to recent critical industry mapping (Havens, Lotz, & Tinic, 2009), analysis of educational broadcasting practices (Perlman, 2010), and research into civic interest programming (Goodman, 2011) by examining how the institutional practices of American public broadcasting developed through the incorporation of hybrid influences such as federal curricular standards and the network' methods of aesthetic production. Such a historical analysis provides insight into the contours of the media reform movement's nascent strategies after 1934. These were conceived not as resistance to national regulation, but moving toward the development of methods centered on meeting the criteria of "public interest" stipulations of the Communications Act for the purpose of expanding educational frequency allocations. The institutional and regulatory origin of public broadcasting in the United States after 1934 must be seen as the manner in which the media reform movement strategically applied multiple influences toward changing communications policy and developing noncommercial genres.

John Studebaker on Public Discourse, Public Forums, and Civic Education

In 1931 Des Moines School Superintendent John Studebaker had applied for and received $125,000 in grants from the Carnegie Corporation to begin a five-year experiment in the Des Moines Public School system for to conduct town-hall-style discussions, which he called "public forums." As Kunzman and Tyack (2005) have written, there were practical reasons to begin this experiment, the most pressing being that an expansion of public participation was viewed as a primary means to mitigate fascism in the United States. But Studebaker (1936c) also worked from a conceptual impulse informed by progressive thought. Over past decades, educators had envisioned the space of public schools as a necessary extension of progressive public service ideals (Goodman, 2011; Reese, 1980). Studebaker considered: if the educational system was to promote training, civic responsibility, and critical democratic discussion, why not expand tactics for democratic participation through free learning among a larger community consortium (Studebaker, 1942)?

To address this question, he developed his concept of the public forum to promote discussion and democratic discourse by "making feasible" a weekly assembly comprised of panels, visual aids, and prepared speeches. Informed by an openly liberalist perspective (Studebaker, 1936c), Studebaker believed that civic education was capable of releasing "the human spirit from the bondage of superstition" and should plant "seeds for freedom" against entrenched powers of the Old World (Studebaker, 1936c). Studebaker argued that freedom of inquiry was best served by a liberal education similar to the scientific method; learning and democratic deliberation should similarly function as trial-and-error processes. Education should be approached as a process that affects future decisions of individual citizens in a democracy, and therefore must concern itself with debunking the notion that any idea or person is infallible through rigorous public questioning (Studebaker, 1936c). "First we teach young children to read and write, second we teach or should teach the young child how to observe the kind of world he lives in, and help him by the use of his tools of learning to discover for himself what is in that world" (Studebaker, 1936c). If public engagement was modeled on a participatory model that included dissent, it would be less likely, he believed, that an unchallenged fascist impulse would appear as a choice in the face of widespread economic or social unrest.

The difference between democracy and fascism, he noted, could be located in the manner in which communication takes place among constituents. At its best, democracy promoted continuous communication of alternate viewpoints, and education was the crucial apparatus for continuous reciprocation between social agents. Public forums were an experiment of a type of Deweyan civic and vocational training in democratic "literacy," and to assist in the development of the "common fund of information and ideas which produce social cohesion" (Studebaker, 1936c). If public communication were continuously reciprocal, he posited, a tradition of discourse and argumentation in a public setting would promote community participation. And such an environment would serve to enervate the emergence of extreme viewpoints such as fascism and turn-of-the-century nativism, because, he wrote, "national unity in a democracy does not imply uniformity of opinion" (Studebaker, 1941). By connecting individuals through shared community interest, a "sympathetic understanding and altruistic spirit" could be realized in the form of communicative responsibility centered on the "educational task" (Studebaker, 1940; see also Goodman, 2011).

The forums were a success in his district, and he buttressed his experiment with an expansion of the forum idea into a Des Moines *Radio School of the Air* in 1934 (Studebaker, 1941) to supplement extant initiatives, whether or not students should be able to attend school or workers able to attend forums or not. As discussed in Paul Clifford Pickett's (1967) dissertation *The Contributions of John Ward Studebaker*, Studebaker's project gained the attention of President Roosevelt and the United States OOE, who sought a new Commissioner. He was granted a one-year appointment that turned into a three-year appointment, and he eventually became the country's longest-serving Commissioner, ending his tenure in 1948 by going into the private sector (Pickett, 1967).

Radio as a National Public Forum: The National Association of Educational Broadcasters meets the Federal Radio Educational Committee

At peak prowess before the Communications Act, there were hundreds of educational broadcasters. The most prominent and well funded were the University of Wisconsin and Ohio State, whose Schools of the Air pulled from progressive stipulations such as the "Wisconsin Idea" that public institutions should make education available to all citizens in a state—especially among otherwise isolated agrarian populations. But in large part, educational broadcasters with less organized administrations had suffered spotty broadcast schedules, misappropriations of the new technology, and wonky equipment. Before the Communications Act, many universities reported that they were unable to make efficient use of their licenses (Crothers to NAEB, 1931; Kadderly, 1932). After the Act, a prominent educational broadcast practitioner echoed the opinion of other remaining stations that an organization would need to rectify past problems by providing basic services to fledgling stations, including an adequate continuity writing bureau to provide acceptable materials and give instructions, sufficient funds to maintain a supplemental system, and, in line with Studebaker's intent, a clearing house to exchange ideas between stations (Beaird to Griffith, 1936). Another letter by a prominent activist lamented that, previous to the Act, "broadcasters had never used the power of radio in their own behalf" (Evans to NAEB, 1938). This sentiment was repeated often after 1934. A 1935 application to the Rockefeller Foundation by the University of Chicago-based University Broadcasting Council argued that a multi-university experiment in "best practices" would be necessary because "educators have achieved so small a part of tremendous social potentialities. While other types of programs have undergone rapid development, those of an educational nature have lagged behind in relatively static conditions. Educational programs have been poorly designed for radio consumption" (Miller, 1935). Internal correspondence began to focus on the strong dichotomy between successful and unsuccessful stations, and it was noted that stations had been separated by the geographic limitations of their broadcast radiuses, preventing the construction of larger learning initiatives (Menzer to McCarty, 1936; Wright to Menzer, McCarty, & Griffith, 1937).

While on the one hand the Ohio School of the Air had received grants from the Payne Fund, and the Carnegie and Rockefeller philanthropic wings had invested in the development of radio curricula (Hilmes, 2011), other university stations received no additional funding and were often run by one or two professors who also had to juggle teaching, research, and administrative duties. When, as Slotten (2000) argues, the Communications Act was passed in favor of medium usage and station ownership, hundreds of well-intentioned but understaffed and underdeveloped stations were handed over to commercial frequencies overnight. Of the couple dozen that remained, in communication through the NAEB, conversations stirred for how to continue with educational broadcasting in spite of new regulation.[1]

There was some dissenting opinion about what course of action to take,[2] but after 1934 members largely agreed: proponents would have to find allies in government. Harold McCarty, an NAEB executive committee member, wrote to Carl Menzer, then president, that it was "important that someone keep an ear to the ground and an eye on the FCC for applications and decisions affecting the interests of the educational stations" (McCarty to Menzer, 1936). Previous to the Act, there was such strong resistance to anything resembling a commercial auspice that most stations had consequently missed that NBC and CBS had, for all of their antagonism to the idea of nonprofit radio, developed aesthetic innovations that not only fascinated radio audiences (Vancour, 2008), but also impressed upon the FRC that their approach was the most streamlined prospect for stable regulation of content and ownership. As Michele Hilmes (1997) wrote, in a very short period of time, network radio constituted a "national imaginary" through rigorous attention to trial-and-error experimentation in style and genre, a centered and focused political lobby, and an understanding of how to disseminate information with clarity. In other words, commercial radio had effectively founded a national imaginary, but they held little inherent interest in promoting democratic ideals. Internal memos at NBC were pejorative at best toward the idea of educational broadcasts and broadcasters (Aylesworth to Reith, 1934); audiences weren't altogether interested in a lecture on physics, NBC President Milton Aylesworth argued, so why should they invest thousands of dollars into broadcasts that would be both unprofitable and unpopular?

One individual stood out to the NAEB as a potential ally. John Studebaker had sent a letter in lieu of attendance to a 1936 conference, stating fidelity to their cause, but arguing that the main difficulty in handling the educational situation was that educators were not agreed upon what they wanted from radio (Studebaker to NAEB, 1936), a problem that educators had already established amongst themselves in private. In 1935, even amongst calls from Congress to set aside educational frequencies, the FCC had recommended against reserved channels (Studebaker to NAEB, 1936). But Studebaker had determined that radio was of crucial importance for the full realization of his idea of national "forums," and began the FREC (Studebaker, 1936a). Studebaker had developed an interest in radio a few years before the Communications Act. By 1935, the commercialization of radio, which shut educators off from propagating public service programming, coupled with the prohibitive cost of running site-based forums with ubiquity, convinced Studebaker that the OOE should take up the question of frequency allocations; there was almost no opportunity for Studebaker to expand his public forum concept onto the airwaves under recent regulation. Formed on December 18, 1935, the FREC was organized as a membership of 40 who met in various subcommittees for the specialized study of educational radio (Studebaker, 1936a). Governance was constructed to include educational, commercial, as well as governmental members. Robert McChesney (1993) previously argued that because of this involvement with commercial interests, the FREC served as a kind of extension of the FRC, which McChesney has correctly argued favored commercial interests during policy making—but Studebaker was not specifically interested in communications policy and took no part in regulatory discussions. Studebaker was an educator who had entered just as the terrain was already set.

Studebaker's strategy was to incorporate members of the still-fledgling NAEB to position educational practitioners for the next set of policy negotiations. He began to update core NAEB members Harold McCarty (Wisconsin), Carl Menzer (Iowa), and Frank Schooley (Illinois) to official positions on major policy and practice issues by the FREC. And he took a decidedly technocratic approach: A 1937 report to the FCC (Studebaker, 1937) argued that an institute for education by radio could maximize the prospects for effective educational broadcasts through cooperative training and workshops between networks and educators. Similarly, in a letter to Rockefeller grant administrator John Marshall, Studebaker argued that the best course of action by proponents would be to streamline educational broadcast standards to satisfy the "public interest" stipulation of the Communications Act (Studebaker to Marshall, 1936). The FREC took the position that for educational broadcasting to flourish, university stations would have to be granted additional budgetary provisions and means of training of radio personnel to improve technical standards (Studebaker, 1936b). Studebaker avoided a national-only approach to advocacy, and contended that radio committees such as the NAEB were necessary to work with governmental associations to create local, state, and regional cooperative broadcasting networks (Studebaker, 1936b) directed at classroom instruction.

The FREC also began to produce lobby pamphlets rich in rhetorical support for educators. Documents argued that recent pioneering experimentation in the classroom, studio, and university radio workshops had stimulated "ferment" en route to solving practical problems of production such as microphone usage or staff training (Studebaker, 1936a). "Its object is to provide the necessary formal structure which will be essential to the eventual creation of a basic and comprehensive plan for the accomplishment of sound education through radio" (Studebaker, 1936a). Widespread mass attunement to the messages of radio had quickly changed the public complexion, and such a vast captive audience demanded variety beyond vaudeville acts, dishwashing liquid commercials, and populist programming. An authoritative body (such as Congress), he posited, should institute safeguards to insure that radio genuinely serve "public interest" beyond proffered pleasures.

Educators at the NAEB were learning to streamline practices, and civic-based public interest programming was immanently plausible. On this, Studebaker wrote, "While entirely sympathetic with the basic aims of educators, broadcasters were cognizant too, of the practical problems with the question involved. Limited funds, lack of training personnel, and the natural preoccupation of educators with education made it improbable, in the opinion of broadcasters, that educators alone could successfully establish and operate stations in the public interests, convenience and necessity, as provided in section B of the Communications Act" (Studebaker, 1936a). Educators previously lacked the production facilities or formal system of training of commercial broadcasters, and suffered "impairment" in productive and economic means.

But advocates anticipated that if FCC standards were met, there should be space for educational broadcasts to function among the dominant model. Educators argued that radio was exerting a powerful educational force whether broadcasters intended it to or not (Studebaker, 1936a), and an educational system would be necessary. After a 1935 conference, the FCC announced its intention that "mutual cooperation between broadcasters and non-profit organizations can be made, to the end of combining the educational experience of the educators, with the program technique of the broadcasters, thereby better to serve the public interest" (Federal Radio Education Committee, 1937). Subsequently, Commissioner James Fly remained open to the idea of expanding educational broadcasting if practitioners were able to provide consistent broadcasts, quality practices, and publicity in line with public interest stipulations. Henceforth, the educational broadcasting practice and reform lobby was directed toward amending the Act by appealing to policy precedent. As Thomas Streeter (1996) argued, such a move can be viewed as a concession to "corporate liberalism," though it's also worth viewing such activity as a tactic by reformers to meet basic criteria of policy to incite later change.

Learning "Best Practice" from the Networks

Through the late 1930s, the OOE began to develop the earliest requirements for "best practices" for educational broadcasts. Among combined initiatives, in the early 1940s, the FREC and NAEB planned to pursue the possible and probable use of FM after the war. The FCC had allowed the NAEB, with vocal support from New York Mayor La Guardia, to rebroadcast educational programs over shortwave radios, as long as those broadcasts were "warped" so as not to be intercepted by foreign ships (FCC release, 1939; Schooley to Studebaker, 1940). More convincingly, in 1938, a band of 25 experimental UHF wavelengths were set aside exclusively for educational broadcasting (Studebaker to Schooley, 1940). Through its interaction with Studebaker, the NAEB continued to clarify its advocacy position at changing established precedents. Writing to Frank Schooley at Illinois, Studebaker suggested that the NAEB draft a strong statement of defense for new allocations. The request, he stipulated, should clearly state how radio would aid instruction directed both to schools and adults (Studebaker, 1940). Schooley's terse statement to the FCC reflected a clear proxy in framing the NAEB's agenda: "I would say we are representatives of institutions of higher learning, engaged in educational broadcasting to promote dissemination of knowledge to the end that both the technical and educational features of broadcasting may be extended to all" (Schooley to Kirwin, 1940). Letters such as Schooley's were drafted with increasing repetition to the FCC, buttressed by new experimental data regarding improved curricular effects of educational radio (Studebaker to Fly, 1944).

Educational advocacy resonated through appeal to the technocratic terms that had won the networks such a monolithic victory in 1934. By the mid-1940s, momentum began to turn toward future frequency allocations for educators. In another letter to FCC Commissioner James Fly, Studebaker wrote that in light of recent progress in educational broadcasting that included exchange of programs, educational channels should be increased to serve an ever-expanding listenership. "Even in those states which might conceivably provide state-wide service within the present band, very little if any leeway can be found for additional stations to serve the special needs of larger city school systems or major centers of higher education" (Studebaker to Fly, 1944). A precedent needed to be set, he argued, so that an advance chain of educational TV channels could be set aside when the technology was ready. In a later 1944 release composed under the rubric Joint Committee on Technical Implementation of Instruction, Studebaker offered a nuanced argument in favor of a permanent segment of educational broadcasting on the national radio band. The American media system, he argued, had reflected the basic philosophy that the individual should be encouraged toward the fullest self-expression constructive to the best interest of civic engagement. The FCC had already administered this "public trust" to the networks. However, the maintenance of the democratic component of the media system demanded freedom for education as much as any other force within the American schema. "The private ownership of property and its administration in the interests of the owner, so long as that administration is not inimical to the public welfare, is a root principle of American philosophy" (Studebaker, 1944). Public education, Studebaker wrote, needed national educational policy to make possible the freedom for every citizen to have "access to learn" (Studebaker, 1944). Since commercial interests had obtained overwhelming ownership of the medium, and since the impact of the spoken word on the radio listener affected the formulation of attitudes of opinion leading to action, commercial interests would need to contribute educational programming, since no national educational radio infrastructure existed (Studebaker, 1944).

Commercial stations half-heartedly pledged cooperation and to "eliminate controversy between educators and commercial broadcasters" (National Association for State Universities, 1936). Noting the FREC's pressure upon the FCC, NBC, and CBS agreed to develop educational broadcasts with the FREC in 1936. Studebaker also arranged for the networks to train educators in broadcast aesthetics as interns. Indeed, networks had always produced high-caliber programming with educational qualities such as NBC's *Music Appreciation Hour* and CBS's *American School of the Air*. With war in Europe looming and a desire to maintain nearly complete ownership of the airwaves, the networks shifted toward educational and nationalistic programs. A Roosevelt-endorsed Educational Radio Project funded three educational radio programs, titled *Struggle for Freedom*, *Let Freedom Ring*, and *Work of the Government*, with $75,000 for an eight-month production window (Studebaker, 1937). And by the end of 1937, due to pressure and funding from Studebaker and the government, the networks produced more than 342 additional programs, many as brief as five minutes, in commercial facilities (Pickett, 1967). Much to everyone's surprise, it was reported that these shows received more than 400,000 letters of support in response, with only 100 of those letters being negative in sentiment. In the build-up to World War II, a total $1,500,000 was spent by the government, commercial stations, and philanthropic organizations on network radio to cover commercial rates, time, and facilities. The enterprise was vast enough that it led to the construction of a complete production unit dedicated to education by radio that included wings for program development, publicity, supplies, and listener mail (Studebaker, 1937).

It is worth noting that while Studebaker was interested in allocations for non-commercial channels, he was willing to work with networks to provide airtime for civic broadcasting. By 1937, educational and network interests began to combine industrial and educational interests for the first time into a national civic production culture with its own economy of scale (Gomery, 1989). Programs were produced to "popularize educational programs for a general audience" (Committee on Radio Education, 1939). And programs were sometimes measured for educational quality with media effects research methods pioneered concurrently by Rockefeller-funded researchers Paul Lazarsfeld, Frank Stanton, and Hadley Cantril (Cantril to Marshall, 1937).

However, this brief period of commercial educational broadcasting was, as Studebaker wrote in a piece titled *The Educational Radio Project and the Office of Education*, a "delicate" relationship that strengthened his conviction to support a noncommercial outlet for educational radio and public education (Cantril to Marshall, 1937). Networks were predictably skeptical that educational programs could continuously attract any number of listeners, but for public relation purposes, they repeatedly stated that they would gladly present educational programs as long as they attracted mass audiences implicit to the network broadcast agenda. So the OOE agreed to allow networks to choose their own staff to develop programs, with notable advisors that included Edward R. Murrow, Dr. Franklin Dunham of NBC, and Studebaker himself. Eventually commercial producers and the OOE seemed to come up with a formula that satisfied both parties. Scripts and plans were devised and sent to committees, changes were made in accordance with suggestions from both educators and entertainers, and initial criticisms compelled both parties to sharpen thinking on the part of program content development. Among these productions, *Democracy in Action*, *I'm an American* and the seminal program *Americans All, Immigrants All* (Savage, 1999) were produced in conjunction with network, FREC, and Smithsonian Institute input.

The OOE, upon completion of a broadcast, would archive all materials, and Studebaker quickly had the Office set up an information exchange program as a "clearing house" for how to adapt educational programming to civic and defense-related purposes. By 1937, a catalog of radio scripts, transcriptions, and recordings—similar to the way that the OOE collected curricular materials—had been prepared and circulated to university educators and school districts. Especially popular were shows that "developed a clear understanding of our democratic heritage and stronger devotion to the democratic cause." Studebaker had constituted a repository and educational script exchange for schools, colleges, and radio stations, distributing more than 80,000 copies in just a couple of years (Studebaker, 1937). Radio workshops, similar to his forum workshops, were operated in cooperation with universities to "profit by the successes and mistakes of the Educational Radio Project." And from this unexpectedly rich period of innovation educators began to constitute an early set of field-wide "best practice." Basic research questions began to be posed for educational broadcasts such as: Does the program have narrative unity? Is the subject matter educationally important? Will the programs effectively induce a considerable proportion of listeners to explore the subject more completely? Is there a summary? The script exchange expanded to cover schools, colleges, and radio stations, and more than 5000 drafts of scripts culminated into a series of 110 usable lessons in regular usage by more than 1500 local independent broadcasters. On average, the production of a half-hour program that utilized all available resources took more than 85 employees and about 2000 hours of work, leading Studebaker to pose a few significant questions that would later substantiate additional educational frequencies: "Can we use techniques for commercial radio for education, can we use commercial radio channels for education, can educational organizations raise enough money to compete for listeners against commercial competition" (Studebaker, 1937)? Most importantly—and least understood by educators during the 1920s—programs selection and presentation of the material was coordinated as such that the *voluntary* interest of the students would continue. As a national forum, accessibility and stimulation of interest became central research questions for all wings of radio pedagogy.

Conclusion: Post-1934 Media Reform Strategies and the Nonmonetary Economy of Public Broadcasting

The media reform movement did not end with the Communications Act. Instead, the addition of new proponents caused a notable shift in organizational approach and political tactics. The period directly after 1934 may be characterized as a transition from the *activist* approach of early reformers to an *advocacy* model. Groups with overlapping fidelity to noncommercial media formed a strategic alliance to increase internal communication and change the available system through lobby, publicity, and technical experimentation. Over a roughly 10-year period, Studebaker was instrumental at early institutionalization of noncommercial media practice and administration. Calling upon FREC strategies and initiatives, NAEB members continued with the FREC's media reform campaign and eventually developed administrative standards and educational genres that influenced noncommercial legislation. Ultimately, NAEB members comprised the first staff of the Corporation for Public Broadcasting (CPB).

Further, the history of American public broadcasting must be differentiated from network broadcasting history. In contrast to the network model of profit and entertainment, advocates built an alternate media system to promote civic paradigms. Through the development of a culture of production and exchange between educators, university practitioners, noncommercial advocates, state and federal bureaucrats, and philanthropic underwriters, media reformers translated a vision of social parity into an infrastructure that thrived as a nonmonetary economy with an entirely different "economy of scale." While recent work on "critical media industries" has primarily focused on mapping for-profit interests, a study of public media *institutions* shows that sustainable broadcasting infrastructures have been constructed via different political, conceptual, productive, and structural determinants than accumulation. The critical distinction between commercial and civic uses of broadcasting technology is first differentiated by intent.

Notes

[1]   Dozens of letters in a series of internal correspondence took place between 1935 and 1938, especially among ranking members W. I. Griffith at Iowa State, Carl Menzer at Iowa, Harold McCarty at Wisconsin, Joseph Wright at Illinois, B. B. Brackett at South Dakota, and affiliated organizations such as the NCER, NACRE, and Rocky Mountain Radio Council; they can be found in the NAEB Papers, Boxes 2, 3, 101, and 110.

[2]   Prominent member Ohio State refused to pay dues in 1937 over disagreement regarding the purpose of the NAEB.

References

Aylesworth, M., to Reith, J., October 8, 1934. NBC Papers, Box 24, Folder 27.

Beaird, to Griffith, W., April 13, 1936. NAEB Papers, Box 2.

Brackett, B., to Beaird, undated 1931. NAEB Papers, Box 1.

Cantril, H., to Marshall, J., May 11, 1937. Rockefeller Archive Center, Box 271, Folder 3233.

Committee on Radio Education, Progressive Education Association memo, May 22, 1939. Rockefeller Archive Center, Box 361, Folder 3719.

Communications Act. Public Law No. 416, June 19, 1934, 73d Congress.

Crothers, to NAEB, regarding revoked license, undated 1931.

Douglas, S. (1987). *Inventing American broadcasting, 1899–1922.* Baltimore, MD: Johns Hopkins University Press.

Evans, H., to NAEB, Bottlenecks in broadcasting, undated 1938. NAEB Papers, Box 2.

FCC release, Hearing for petition by Mayor La Guardia, undated 1939. NAEB Papers, Box 2.

Federal Radio Education Committee, internal memo, January 12, 1937. Rockefeller Archive Center, Box 332, Folder 3951.

Gomery, D. (1989). Media economics: Terms of analysis. *Critical Studies in Mass Communication, 6,* 43–60. doi:10.1080/15295038909366730

Goodman, D. (2011). *Radio's civic ambition: American broadcasting and democracy in the 1930s.* New York, NY: Oxford Press.

Havens, T., Lotz, A., & Tinic, S. (2009). Critical media industry studies: A research approach. *Communication, Culture, Critique, 2*(2), 234–253. doi:10.1111/j.1753-9137.2009.01037.x

Hilmes, M. (1997). *Radio voices: American broadcasting, 1922–1952.* Minneapolis, MN: University of Minnesota Press.

Hilmes, M. (2011). *Network nations: A transnational history of British and American broadcasting.* New York, NY: Routledge.

Kadderly, in NAEB Bulletin, April 14, 1932. NAEB Papers, Box 19.

Kirkpatrick, B. (2006). Localism in American media policy, 1920–1934: Reconsidering a "bedrock concept." *Radio Journal: International Studies in Broadcast and Audio Media, 4*(1–3), 87–110.

Kunzman, R., & Tyack, D. (2005). Educational forums of the 1930s: An experiment in adult civic education. *American Journal of Education, 111*(3), 320–340. doi:10.1086/428884

McCarty, H., to Menzer, C., April 13, 1936. NAEB Papers, Box 2.

McChesney, R. W. (1993). *Telecommunications, mass media, and democracy: The battle for the control of U.S. broadcasting, 1928–1935*. New York, NY: Oxford University Press.

Menzer, C., to McCarty, H., December 3, 1936. NAEB Papers, Box 2.

Miller, A.The problem of educational broadcasting and a plan for its solution, Undated 1935. Submitted to John Marshall at the Rockefeller Foundation, Rockefeller Archive Center, Box 284, Folder 3394.

Mitchell, J. (2005). *Listener supported: The culture and history of public radio*. New York, NY: Praeger.

NAEB Bulletin, February 20, 1931. NAEB Papers, Box 19.

NAEB Membership Ledgers, 1935–1937. NAEB Papers, Box 2.

National Association for State Universities, November 1936. NAEB Papers, Box 2.

Ohio State Radio Institute Conference Proceedings, 1934. NAEB Papers, Box 19; Preamble to the constitution for the National Association for Educational Broadcasters, NAEB Papers, Box 1.

Perlman, A. (2010). Televisions up in the air: The Midwest program on airborne television instruction, 1959–1971. *Critical Studies in Media Communication*, *27*(5), 477–497. doi:10.1080/15295030903583655

Pickett, P. C. (1967). The contributions of John Ward Studebaker. Doctoral Dissertation. University of Iowa, Iowa City.

Reese, W. (1980). *Power and promise of school reform*. New York, NY: Teacher College.

Savage, B. (1999). Broadcasting freedom: Radio, war and politics of race, 1938–1948. Chapel Hill, NC: University of North Carolina Press.

Schooley, F., to Kirwin, T., undated 1940. Princeton Radio Project, FREC Papers.

Slotten, H. (2000). *Radio and television regulation: Broadcast technology in the United States, 1920–1960*. Baltimore, MD: Johns Hopkins University Press.

Slotten, H. (2009). *Radio's hidden voice: The origins of public broadcasting in the United States*. Urbana, IL: University of Illinois Press.

Smulyan, S. (1994). *Selling radio: The commercialization of American broadcasting, 1920–1934*. Washington, DC: Smithsonian Institution Press.

Streeter, T. (1996). *Selling the air*. Chicago, IL: University of Chicago Press.

Studebaker, J., to Fly, J., undated 1944. Princeton Radio Project, FREC Paper.

Studebaker, J., to Marshall, J., December 12, 1936. Rockefeller Archive Papers, Box 332, Folder 3950.

Studebaker, J., to NAEB, undated 1936. NAEB Papers, Box 19.

Studebaker, J., to Schooley, F., undated 1940. Princeton Radio Project, FREC Papers.

Studebaker, J. (1936a). *The federal radio education committee*. Washington, DC: Office of Education.

Studebaker, J. (1936b). *Report of the radio committee to the national association of state universities*. Washington, DC: Office of Education.

Studebaker, J. (1936c). *Plain talk*. Washington, DC: National Home Library Foundation.

Studebaker, J. (1937). *The educational radio project of the office of education*. Washington, DC: Office of Education.

Studebaker, J. (1940b). *Twentieth century educational approaches in the use of communication*. Washington, DC: Office of Education.

Studebaker, J. (1941a). *Classification of educational radio research. Report of the federal radio education committee*. Washington, DC: Office of Education.

Studebaker, J. (1942). *On managing meetings for freedom forums*. Washington, DC: Office of Education.

Studebaker, J. (1944). *Report of the joint committee on technical implementation of instruction*. Washington, DC: Office of Education.

Vancour, S. (2008). The sounds of radio. Doctoral Dissertation. University of Wisconsin–Madison, Madison, WI.

Wright, J., to Menzer, C., McCarty, H., & Griffith, W., October 1937. NAEB Papers, Box 2.

Archives:

Princeton University, Princeton Radio Project Papers: Pamphlets on Education in the United States. FREC Papers.

Rockefeller Archive Center: RF Files, Boxes 24, 236, 254, 264, 271, 332, 359.

University of Maryland–College Park. Library of American Broadcasting, Public Broadcasting Archives. Association for Educational Communications and Technology Papers: Boxes 3, 4, 6.

University of Wisconsin–Madison, Wisconsin Center for Film and Theater Research: National Association of Educational Broadcasters Papers, Boxes 1, 2, 3, 4, 19, 101, 102, 110.

Be Realistic, Demand the Impossible: Three Radically Democratic Internet Policies

Robert W. McChesney

The policies surrounding the Internet in the United States are determined by what the wealthiest and most powerful players wish to have happen. This is producing a digital world that is inimical to democracy and to the revolutionary potential of these technologies. The author argues for radical policies: the nationalization of the ISP/cellphone industry and its conversion to a public utility; the nationalization of huge Internet monopolies that are impervious to antitrust; the adoption of a massive public subsidy to pay for independent, competitive, uncensored, noncommercial news media. The author points out that these proposals have a basis in conservative theory as well as radical and liberal democratic theory. It is imperative to broaden the debate and draw the citizenry into it.

In this article I propose three policy ideas to make the internet a force for democracy in the U.S., and potentially worldwide. These are radical ideas, far outside the existing range of debate inside political circles or even the academy. My unorthodox approach rests on a series of propositions:

First, the internet has developed as it has largely as a result of policies; there is no such thing as a natural "default" course of development. That it switched from being an anti-commercial, egalitarian institution in the early 1990s to a "whoever makes the most money by any means necessary wins" undertaking was not foreordained by the gods. It was the province of politics (McChesney, 2013).

Second, the internet has become a, if not *the*, dominant force in modern capitalism. Three of the four most valuable publicly traded corporations in the U.S.

are internet-related firms, and 13 of the 32 most valuable firms are primarily internet firms (iWeblist, 2014). By contrast, only three of the "too big to fail" banks—which Senator Richard Durbin (D-IL), in reference to Congress, concedes "frankly own the place"—rank among the 32 most valuable firms in the economy (Grim, 2009).

Third, U.S. capitalism is in the midst of what Paul Krugman refers to as another Great Depression. Unemployment remains very high, corporations are sitting on some $1.7 trillion that they do not invest in new plants and equipment, and downward pressures on wages, particularly for the working class, are extreme ("Labour pains," 2013). Consequently, poverty rates have returned to levels not seen for nearly a century in the U.S., and inequality in the U.S. is trending toward that found in Malaysia or the Philippines, with western Europe and Japan in its rearview mirror (Abramsky, 2013). Nothing in the range of current debates on economic policy proposes anything that will change this dynamic.

Fourth, the U.S. political system has become what John Nichols and I characterize as a "Dollarocracy" (Nichols and McChesney, 2013). The vast majority of the population has no influence over core policies, regulations, taxation, or the budget, which are the province of large corporations and the very wealthy, who dominate American governance (Gilens, 2005, 2012; Schlozman, Verba, & Brady, 2012; Bartels, 2008; Hacker & Pierson, 2010). Systemic corruption is the order of the day. The election system has been rendered largely ineffective as a means for citizens to engage in self-government. As former president Jimmy Carter said in 2013, the U.S. is no longer a "functioning democracy" (Riva, 2013).

These above propositions are closely related. They lead to a final proposition: The current political economy situation in the U.S. is unstable and ultimately untenable. When one factors in the environmental crisis, this becomes an even more calamitous and desperate period (Klein, 2013). In the past 150 years the U.S. has had several moments of major reform—Reconstruction, the Progressive Era, the New Deal, and the 1960s—in which social upheaval led to sweeping changes being enacted that made the country more democratic and addressed growing inequality and corruption. When such reform periods do emerge—what have been termed *critical junctures*—all the major institutions in society are subject to criticism in a manner that does not exist in more stable times. What had been regarded as impossible becomes realistic.

Nobody can predict the future, so I cannot guarantee that the U.S. is on the verge of such a reform period. But I can say the conditions are ripe by historical standards, and in my view the U.S. desperately needs such an era of fundamental reform, arguably equal to or greater than any in the nation's history. Hence it is incumbent upon all who cherish democratic values to work toward encouraging such a period. One way to do that is to cast our vision for how society can be structured far beyond what is permissible to the existing rulers of the political economy. In the second decade of the 21st century in the U.S., that means directly challenging the existing internet regime. Unless we can begin to imagine the impossible, it may never become realistic.

First Proposal: End the ISP Cartel

Back in the 1990s much verbiage was expended about how the internet would unleash such a ferocious wave of competition between the Baby Bell telephone companies, the long-distance providers, and the cable TV companies that government regulation (of what were mostly licensed monopolies) in the public interest was no longer necessary. The market could work its magic in combination with the digital revolution, which made competition seemingly endless. There were roughly 15 major Baby Bell, long-distance, and cable/satellite TV companies in 1996, and, it was said, they were raring to take each other's business if they were freed from government regulations. These firms also said they needed to be unchained because scores of new competitors were about to capitalize on the possibilities of digital technology and come after their markets.

These claims constituted one of the largest piles of horse manure in American political history. The dominant firms that pushed this line of reasoning knew they could game the system sufficiently to all but eliminate the threat of real competition, and they could use the relaxation of rules to greatly increase their market power (Wu, 2010). In 2013, there were only a half-dozen or so major players that dominated the provision of broadband internet access and wireless internet access. Three of them—Verizon, AT&T, and Comcast—dominate the field of telephony and internet access, and have set up what is in effect a cartel. They no longer compete with each other in any meaningful sense. As a result, Americans pay far more for cellphone and broadband internet access than most other advanced nations and get much lousier service. "They're making a ton of money," one telecommunication executive said about the cartel members in 2013. "They're picking the pockets of consumers" (Greeley & Moritz, 2013).

These are not "free market" companies in any sense of the term. Their business model going back to pre-internet days has always been to capture government monopoly licenses for telephone and cable TV services. Their "comparative advantage" has never been customer service; it has been world-class lobbying. It was that power that made it possible for them to endlessly merge into corporate goliaths and permitted them to quietly overturn existing regulations a decade ago so they could monopolize their networks for broadband internet access. That killed competition once and for all. The remaining public interest regulations these behemoths face today are laughable.

The public interest community has responded in a number of ways. One policy response has been to press for Network Neutrality, which would prevent the cartel from using its monopoly power to censor websites. (If there were actual competition, the policy would be unnecessary because consumers would be unlikely to select an internet service provider [ISP] that engaged in censorship.) Another response has been for communities to set up their own local municipally run broadband services— a public option, if you will. Wherever the cartel has not been able to crush these efforts, the municipal broadband services have proven highly popular. But they are in a constant battle for survival as the cartel uses its considerable lobbying muscle to try to outlaw them.

The cartel has passed its historical expiration date. These firms are parasites that use their government-created monopoly power to exact economic "rents"—by which economists mean undeserved income—from consumers and other businesses. Let's pay them a fair price for their equipment and cash them out. Then let's make cellphone and broadband access ubiquitous and as close to free as possible. (And, by doing so, we could stop paying through our teeth for satellite TV and cable TV services as well.) How to structure a publicly owned nonprofit network, a digital post office, is exactly where study, debate, and discussion should be directed. It is a solvable problem and one that demands immediate attention.

Ironically, although socialists and progressives have traditionally liked this approach to telecommunication, this is an idea with considerable resonance in the business community as well, as other firms are tired of paying a ransom to the cartel for crappy service. Google launched its own broadband service in Kansas City, if only to demonstrate how it would be possible to have a vastly superior broadband network if the cartel simply got off its butt and invested some of its mega-profits into it. In 2008 then-Google executive and legendary internet architect Vint Cerf asked publicly whether the internet might not be better if the data-pipe infrastructure were "owned and maintained by the government, just like the highways" (Schonfeld, 2008). It is a serious question that demands a serious answer.

Second Proposal: Treat Monopolies like ... Monopolies

One of the reasons the internet boom has not led to a golden age of investment and prosperity in contemporary capitalism—unlike, say, what followed from the emergence of the automobile and all of its many related industries in the twentieth century—is that much of the wealth generated by the internet has been funneled into a very small number of hands. Aside from the cartel, which was an outgrowth of the old telecommunication monopolies, the internet has produced monopolistic titans like Google, Apple, Amazon, Facebook, eBay, Microsoft, Intel, Cisco, Oracle, and Qualcomm.

These firms take advantage first and foremost of network effects, which tend to produce "winner-take-all" markets and where there tends to be almost no middle class of mid-sized firms. In addition, patent law and traditional economies of scale contribute to insurmountable advantages over potential adversaries. Indeed, increasingly the internet seems like a walled garden where these giants are battling with each other for domination in existing and prospective markets, and no one else has a prayer, except to get bought out by a giant. In 2013 the head of the Wikimedia Foundation, which operates the ubiquitous nonprofit and noncommercial Wikipedia, stated that it would be impossible for Wikipedia or anything like it to be created and thrive on the internet today due to the dominance of the internet monopolies (Sue Gardner, personal communication, October 22, 2013). The system is locked down.

In combination, these firms have virtually unassailable power in Washington, and the only time they face any regulatory threat is when the giants find themselves on opposite sides of an issue, as has happened with Network Neutrality and intellectual property debates. These firms tend to get glowing press coverage, and their executives and largest investors are regarded like celebrities or championship athletes; the idea that these firms' legitimacy might be challenged probably seems preposterous to all but a few.

But these are all monopolies in the sense that economists use the term: they control sufficient market share—usually at least 50 or 60%—to determine pricing and to determine how much competition they have. As such they pose a direct threat not only to smaller enterprises but to democratic governance. This, again, is not exclusively a belief held by socialists and progressives; it has been at various times a staple belief of conservative free market economic theory.

No less a figure than Milton Friedman argued that capitalism was superior for political freedom and democracy because it separated political power from economic power, unlike feudalism or communism, under which the people who controlled the economy also controlled the politics (Friedman, 1962). One of Friedman's mentors at the University of Chicago, the laissez faire champion Henry C. Simons, said it was imperative that private firms not be allowed to become too large and monopolistic for this argument to hold (Simons, 1948). Giant monopolistic firms kyboshed the ability of capitalism to remain democratic, because the large firms would overwhelm governance. Here Simons was in agreement with his periodic adversary President Franklin Roosevelt, who in a 1938 message to Congress stated: "The first truth is that the liberty of a democracy is not safe if the people tolerate the growth of private power to a point where it becomes stronger than their democratic state itself. That, in its essence, is fascism—ownership of government by an individual, by a group, or by any other controlling private power" (Roosevelt, 1942).

Simons argued that it was imperative—for both genuine free enterprise and democracy—that monopolistic firms either be broken into much smaller competitive units or be "socialized" and directed by the government in a transparent manner (Simons, 1948). Because network effects make it nearly impossible to imagine the effective breakup of the internet giants, Simons's analysis points squarely in one direction. It is high time we take seriously his concerns and think about how the monopolized internet services could be put in the public domain, and guided by open-source protocol.

One immediate benefit of this approach: the incessant commercial pressure to collect every possible bit of information on users to better manipulate them would be undermined. It would be far easier to have a regimen with standards closer to what was imagined by the engineers who created the internet: power would be in the hands of the users, who would control their own digital fate, rather than in the hands of giant firms that are mostly unaccountable ... except to their investors.

Third Proposal: Treat Journalism Like a Public Good

Perhaps the greatest irony or unexpected consequence of the internet has been that, notwithstanding all its democratizing contributions, it has not ushered in a Golden Age of journalism and culture. Instead of unlimited quality and quantity, the internet has eliminated most of the resources that once went to support content production. What I write in this section applies to the entirety of culture, but I will focus specifically on journalism.

As an institution, journalism is in freefall collapse in the U.S. There are vastly fewer paid reporters and editors than there were a generation ago, and it is especially striking when you consider how much the population has grown in that time. Most newsrooms look like the Polish countryside in 1945. Much of what government does, and government's interactions with commercial interests, receives much less coverage than they did in the past. Most elections are uncovered, and what paid campaign journalism remains hardly makes one pine for more of the same. This process began before the internet, but the internet has accelerated the process and has made it permanent.

Why is this a problem? All democratic theory, as well as the specific history of the American republic, is premised on the idea that democracy requires an informed, participating citizenry, and such a citizenry can only exist with strong and vibrant journalism. If such journalism does not exist, our republic and our freedoms cannot survive in any meaningful sense. It is not an exaggeration to say that this point was an obsession for the nation's founders, in particular Thomas Jefferson and James Madison (McChesney, 2013; McChesney & Nichols, 2010).

Why is journalism disintegrating? Commercial interests have decided that journalism is no longer a viable investment, and they are jumping ship. When Jeff Bezos reached into his spare change jar to purchase the *Washington Post* for $250 million in 2013, he paid perhaps 5% of what the purchase price would have been in 2000. Ironically, for the past two decades, as the commercial interest in journalism has shriveled, the conventional wisdom has been that the internet would eventually replace dying old media with digital commercial journalism that would likely be far superior to what it replaced. We just had to be patient and let good old Yankee ingenuity, magical technologies, and the profit motive solve the problem.

But that hasn't happened, nor will it. Indeed, what remains of paid journalism in the U.S. is disproportionately in "old media." The internet has been a total flop. If anything, by giving the illusion of an information rainforest with every Google search, it has made people oblivious to the actual information desert we increasingly inhabit.

Why is that? Advertising provided the vast majority of revenues for journalism in the twentieth century and made doing news media commercially lucrative. Advertisers needed to help pay for journalism to attract readers/viewers to news media who would then see their ads. That was the deal. Advertisers supported the news because they had no other choice if they wished to achieve their commercial goals; they had no intrinsic attachment to the idea of a free press. The rise of advertising as the primary basis of support prompted the development of professional journalism, in part to protect the content of the news from direct commercial influence; advertising generally was regarded as a necessary evil for the subsidization of journalism.

But those debates are now passé. In the new era of smart or targeted digital advertising, advertisers no longer place ads on specific websites and hope to appeal to whoever might visit the website. Instead, they purchase target audiences directly and place ads through internet ad networks that locate the desired target wherever they are online. *Advertisers no longer need to support journalism or content creation at all.* This is probably why Rupert Murdoch, the greatest corporate media visionary of our times, abandoned his iPad/smart phone news venture, *The Daily*, in 2012; it is definitely why the *Guardian*, one of the most visited and venerated news websites in the world, concedes that it has no idea how it can support its operations when and if it is forced to rely upon internet revenues.

Advertising gave the illusion that journalism is a naturally, even supremely, commercial endeavor. But when advertising disappears, journalism's true nature comes into focus: it is a public good, something society requires but that the market cannot provide in sufficient quality or quantity. Like other public goods, if society wants it, it will require public policy and public spending. There is no other way.

This evidence points overwhelmingly in this direction. Every year the magazine *The Economist* ranks all the nations of the world according to how democratic they are. Every year those nations that top the list are invariably the nations that spend the most per capita on public and community media. Freedom House, another mainstream organization, annually ranks all the nations of the world in terms of how free their press systems are. Government censorship is the single threat Freedom House is most concerned about. Every year the same nations that rank atop *The Economist*'s list rule Freedom House's list of the freest and best press systems. The truth is this: in democratic nations, journalism subsidies tend to make the press more diverse and dissident and critical of the government in power. Like education, it is a public good, and, as with education, the more resources that are devoted to it, the better it will be, everything else being equal.

There is one outstanding question: How did the U.S. have a press system that was the envy of the world in the nineteenth century prior to the advent of mass advertising? It did so by having massive postal and printing subsidies for newspapers, which made the cost of production so low that there were many more newspapers per capita than anywhere else in the world. In the first century of American history, our politicians did not know the term "public good," but they treated the press in precisely that manner.

If we are going to remain a republic, we need journalism, and that requires massive public support. All attention should be on devising and debating the sorts of policies and subsidies that would produce the optimum results and prevent any form of government censorship of favoritism. It is a solvable problem, but only if we are willing to face the issue honestly.

One idea I like: Dean Baker's notion (which I have embellished) of letting every American over the age of 18 direct up to $200 every year to any nonprofit medium of his or her choice. The only conditions would be that the recipient be a recognized nonprofit, that the recipient take no commercial advertising, and that whatever is produced by the subsidy be posted online immediately and enter the public domain.

It would not be protected by copyright. This would amount to a $30 billion public investment with no government control over who gets the money. This would promote all sorts of competition as well, as entities would be competing for the monies.

There are probably many other ways we could support a great free press system (and a great culture) in the digital era. It is high time to start that discussion.

References

Abramsky, S. (2013). *The American way of poverty: How the other half still lives.* New York, NY: Nation Books.

Bartels, L.M. (2008). *Unequal democracy.* New York, NY: Russell Sage Foundation.

Friedman, M. (1962). *Capitalism and freedom.* Chicago, IL: University of Chicago Press.

Gilens, M. (2005). Inequality and democratic responsiveness. *Public Opinion Quarterly, 69*(5), 778–796. Retrieved from http://dx.doi.org/10.1093/poq/nfi058

Gilens, M. (2012). *Affluence and influence: Economic inequality and political power in America.* Princeton, NJ: Princeton University Press.

Greeley, B., & Moritz, S. (2013, November 4–10). Bananas: How T-Mobile plans to survive by blowing up one of the most profitable business models around. *Bloomberg Businessweek,* p. 66.

Grim, R. (2009, May 30). Dick Durbin: Banks "frankly own the place." Retrieved from http://www.huffingtonpost.com/2009/04/29/dick-durbin-banks-frankly_n_193010.html

Hacker, J.S., & Pierson, P. (2010). *Winner-take-all politics: How Washington made the rich richer— and turned its back on the middle class.* New York, NY: Simon & Schuster.

iWeblist (2014). U.S. commerce—stock market capitalization of the 50 largest American companies. Retrieved from http://www.iweblists.com/us/commerce/MarketCapitalization.html

Klein, N. (2013, October 29). How science is telling us all to revolt. Retrieved from http://www.newstatesman.com/2013/10/science-says-revolt

Labour pains: Workers' share of national income. (2013). *The Economist, 409*(8856), pp. 77–78.

McChesney, R.W. (2013). *Digital disconnect: How capitalism is turning the internet against democracy.* New York, NY: The New Press.

McChesney, R.W., & Nichols, J. (2010). *The death and life of American journalism: The media revolution that will begin the world again.* New York, NY: Nation Books.

Nichols, J., & McChesney, R.W. (2013). *Dollarocracy: How the money and media election complex is destroying America.* New York, NY: Nation Books.

Riva, A. (2013, July 18). Jimmy Carter: U.S. "has no functioning democracy." Retrieved from http://www.salon.com/2013/07/18/jimmy_carter_us_has_no_functioning_democracy_partner/

Roosevelt, F.D. (1942, June). Appendix A: Message from the president of the U.S. transmitting recommendations relative to the strengthening and enforcement of anti-trust laws. *The American Economic Review, 32*(2), pt. 2, Supplement: Papers Relating to the Temporary National Economic Committee, 119–128.

Schlozman, K.L., Verba, S., & Brady, H. E. (2012). *The unheavenly chorus: Unequal political voice and the broken promise of American democracy.* Princeton, NJ: Princeton University Press.

Schonfeld, E. (2008, June 25). Vint Cerf wonders if we need to nationalize the internet. Retrieved from http://techcrunch.com/2008/06/25/vint-cerf-wonders-if-we-need-to-nationalize-the-internet/

Simons, H.C. (1948). *Economic policy for a free society.* Chicago, IL: University of Chicago Press.

Wu, T. (2010). *The master switch: The rise and fall of information empires.* New York, NY: Knopf.

Hyper-power and Private Monopoly: The Unholy Marriage of (Neo)corporatism and the Imperial Surveillance State

Chris Marsden

American hyper-power world dominance by public and private agencies has replaced British Empire hyper-power world domination in the period 1815–1914. Edward Snowden's revelations of United States and United Kingdom surveillance have given rise to several important papers examining the geographical and territorial limits of the internet, comparing it to the imperial telegraph and even to the Roman imperial road. This paper recalls earlier telegraphy research and explains how the previous hyper-power, the British Empire, was able to control communications in order to extend its extraterritorial application of domestic law. I explain that the nineteenth century telegraph 'cables that girdled the Earth' were sunk into the sea in Cornwall, southwest England, and that today's internet fibre cables are in the same places – with the result that the greatest National Security Agency espionage-gathering operation is a joint US/UK operation from the small town of Bude, Cornwall. Add to that historical espionage the invention of encryption/decryption computing, devices from Babbage's Difference Engine to Turing and Tommy Flower's Colossus Marks I and II that broke both Enigma and Lorenz in World War II. The recipe now exists for what the National Security Agency calls 'Total Information Awareness' and the Orwellian nightmare of totally efficient surveillance and 'war is peace' according to the Ministry of Truth. But it existed before, and we should learn from the past.

It is unprecedented, claimed the Europeans, Asians, Africans, and Latin Americans. How could the Americans spy on us—and the British in their wake (Gustin, 2013)? This has never happened before, and must never happen again. Comparisons were made to the East German Stasi and the Soviet KGB, perhaps forgetting the extraordinary undersea cable surveillance conducted by the U.S. against the Soviet Union in the 1970s (Khazan, 2013). But the real comparison is to the Eastern Telegraph Company and its offshoots in the Eastern Hemisphere, and International Telephone & Telegraph (ITT: Sampson, 1973) in the Western. American hyper-power world dominance by public and private agencies has replaced British Empire hyper-power world domination in the period 1815–1914. Snowden's revelations have given rise to several important papers examining the geographical and territorial limits on the internet, comparing it to the imperial telegraph (Kurbalija, 2013) and even to the Roman imperial road (Moglen, 2013).

This paper recalls earlier telegraphy research (Kennedy, 1971, Barty-King, 1980; Standage, 1999; Hills, 2007) and explains how the previous hyper-power (Marsden, 2004, describing a global super-power without effective opposition, from the French *hyper-puissance*) was able to control communications in order to extend its extraterritorial application of domestic law. I explain that the telegraph 'cables that girdled the Earth' (Clarke, 1958) were sunk into the sea in Cornwall, southwest England, and that today's internet fiber cables are in the same places—with the result that the greatest National Security Agency espionage-gathering operation is a joint U.S./U.K. operation from the small town of Bude, Cornwall. Add to that historical espionage the invention of encryption/decryption computing, devices from Babbage's Difference Engine to Turing and Tommy Flower's Colossus Marks I and II that broke both Enigma and Lorenz in World War II.[1]

The recipe now exists for what the National Security Agency calls "Total Information Awareness" and the Orwellian nightmare of totally efficient surveillance and "war is peace" according to the Ministry of Truth.[2] But it existed before, and we should learn from the past.

Cabling, Surveillance and the Spread of Western Capitalism

The British Empire was built by a miniscule nation-state, with enormous private corporations developing first the West Indies and Americas, famously rescinding economic growth in these territories when new opportunities in the east and south arose in the nineteenth century. The extraordinary British Navy sought and gained dominance of the North Atlantic in the Seven Years (1756–1763) and Napoleonic Wars (1792–1815; EurActiv, 2013), with a largish blip in what the U.S. calls the Revolutionary Wars, but was in reality an Anglo-French war by proxy (Earle, 2004).[3] From the invention of the Monroe Doctrine in 1823, the Anglo-American powers were to hold the world's balance of communications power, especially after their destruction of the great majority of the Iberian and Chinese empires by 1898. Simon de Bolivar may have wrested independence from Spain in the 1820s, but he recognized that the U.S. and Great Britain controlled the sea lanes that connected Latin America to markets in Europe and Asia.[4]

Two vital legal innovations enabled this increasing global control of trade on behalf of the Empire (Muchlinski, 2007, pp. 8, 34). The first was the invention of the joint stock corporation. The second legal innovation was the direct enforcement of English law across the globe.

The joint stock corporation enabled capital raising in London on an enormous scale, first to provide the investment in domestic railways which transformed the industrial and commercial base in the U.K., a trick accomplished in large part by the year of revolutions (and economic collapse): 1848. Repeating the trick elsewhere was child's play (and many heirs' fortunes were fleeced by unscrupulous prospectus fiction authors), and the British built railways all over the world, including across South America as well as in the colonies. This stock raising was a vital extension of the directors' direct duties and investment which had enabled a more controlled stock growth in the great British East India Company (and its French, Dutch, Danish, and other equivalents). The British corporation unleashed wars of Christian-moralist-fuelled occupation on Bengal then on the rest of India, pausing only when the whole of India was under their Wellington boot, with tightly controlled local dictators (the maharajahs) in place wherever possible, controlled by a British 'Resident' (equivalent to a U.S. super-ambassador such as in Cairo, Kabul, or Baghdad: James, 1998).[5] The British invaded Afghanistan in 1838 (and on many other occasions) and helped create the heroin industry in that benighted country. British India was a captive market for those and other products. The British used corporate-financed fighters: mercenaries, special forces and privateers.[6] In the 'Opium Wars' of 1839–1842 and 1856–1860, the British forces defeated the Chinese government to allow British corporations to sell opium on the free market. British forces occupied Hong Kong Island from 1841 to 1997 and controlled Shanghai and other coastal cities for much of this time, benefitting other rapacious foreign powers such as the US, Germany and Japan. The British corporations also occupied and stocked with Chinese "bonded labor" (slaves in all but name) the Malay archipelago, even installing a 'White Rajah' adventurer in Borneo.

The second legal innovation was the direct enforcement of English law across the globe, and this enforcement is best exemplified by the Africa Squadron of the British Navy, which fought to enforce anti-slavery law against U.S. slavers on the open seas.[7] The financing of the Suez Canal by the British government (Egyptian government bought out 1875; occupation of the canal zone completed 1888), and Panama by the U.S., completed their encirclement of the globe, which they had girdled with telegraph cables (Clarke, 1958). Throughout the period, the British were tightening their grip on the route to the East, via both the Suez and the Cape of Good Hope (the invasion of the Boer Republic completing that occupation in 1902).

Military-Industrial Information Governance in the Telegraph Era

Early industrial innovations were to blossom in the second half of the nineteenth century, when the great genius Isambard Kingdom Brunel's innovations would confirm Britain's place as the first truly global power.[8] The last sheltered beach at the extreme southwest of England is Porthcurno, a beach which was the center of the surveillance intelligence complex of the British Empire and today houses a museum to that communications power.[9] Cornish beaches still serve a vital function in two legal rights. First, many beach foreshores are the property of the Duchy of Cornwall,[10] the Duke being the heir to the English (and thus Cornish) throne and still the sole arbiter of Crown prerogative at landing sites.[11] Second, these cables connect Europe to Africa, Asia, and the Americas via that extraordinary dominance of high-value communications controlled by a British company that became even greater in its own way than those of Brunel or the British East India Company. That company is now Cable & Wireless, or the Eastern Telegraph Company as it was then known (Barty-King, 1980). The telegraph line that ran alongside every railway in the period after electrical telegraphy's invention in 1837[12] was realized to be capable of intercontinental reach.[13] The prize achieved in 1866 was the ability to communicate in nearly real time between the great commercial centers of London and New York, and eventually to all the railheads that the joint stock companies were building into the Argentine pampas, the Himalayan hill stations, and the red heart of Australia. With that dot-dash information came control and power, both corporate and governmental.

This prize was of inestimable commercial value—such that no serious obstacle to capital raising was ever encountered after the proof of concept cable to the Americas was first built and tested. Military and surveillance value was even greater. Consider the Indian Rebellion of 1857, which laid to rest the direct corporate rule of India by the East India Company, the British Crown taking over formal responsibility. But it took so long to relay information about the fighting, that it was evident that radical reform of communication to India and China was required. Werner von Siemens first achieved the feat via land, closely followed by Charles Bright's Eastern Telegraph (Kimberlin, 1994). Bright then laid the 1870 Bombay submarine cable, 1872 Singapore-Shanghai/Australia cable and 1872 merger that created the Eastern Telegraph Company. Glover argues that "The Indo-European submarine cable and the formation of the Eastern Telegraph Company are one and the same story" (Glover, 2011). British Prime Minister Disraeli in 1875 bought a controlling interest in Frenchman Ferdinand de Lessep's Suez Canal—which would condemn Egypt and much of the Gulf and Red Sea to British military occupation for over 80 years in the interests of British shipping and the cable. Note that the first trans-Pacific cable was only operationalized in 1903, using British-controlled Fanning Island rather than Hawaii to maintain the "all-red" system of cable landing stations within the Empire (Kennedy, 1971).

Even where commercial interest had not laid a cable, military need would help the march of the joint stock corporation. The longest undersea cable prior to the failed 1857 Atlantic cable was laid by the Anglo-French Expeditionary Force across the Black Sea to the Crimean Peninsula in 1854 (Kimberlin, 1994). The failed Rhodes-funded Jameson Raid on the gold and diamond-rich Transvaal Republic in 1895 led rapidly to the full military invasion of the Transvaal on October 11, 1899, and the invention of the concentration camp (the British 'Guantànamo') to control the Boer families' loyalty. The Boer War needed more British telegraphs than then existed too, as Glover (2011) details. The speed of construction in the mid-Atlantic shows the efficiency and reach of the Eastern Telegraph Company (ETC), and with it the British Empire, only 40 years after the first successful undersea cable. Together with the "all-red" imperial undersea cable routes, a virtual monopoly on corporate cable-laying (and therefore cutting) ships in the service of the Eastern Telegraph Company and her siblings, and the extraordinary advantage of the Royal Navy protecting landing stations, this ensured British cable security—and the insecurity of other commercial-imperial links. At the outbreak of World War I in 1914, German communication cables were immediately cut, and the Navy sank German cable-destroyer *SMS Emden* in the Cocos Islands, leaving only Fanning Island briefly vulnerable to the German Pacific fleet (Kennedy, 1971). With Navy-approved censors on all landing stations and operators approved by the wartime censors, preventing encrypted communications being sent, Germany was largely cut off from her Empire within weeks of war breaking out. Wireless telegraphy was both less secure and technologically immature in this period, though it would predominate as a means of German telegraphy by 1939, with Enigma machine encryption and its heroic hacking by the Bletchley Park digital computing team inspired by Alan Turing.

Whistle blowers also have a long history. As explained to the most recent Sam Addams award winner, Edward Snowden, at his awards ceremony:

> in 1773, Benjamin Franklin leaked confidential information by releasing letters written by then-Lt. Governor of Massachusetts Thomas Hutchinson to Thomas Whatley, an assistant to the British Prime Minister. The letters suggested that it was impossible for the colonists to enjoy the same rights as subjects living in England and that "an abridgement of what are called English liberties" might be necessary. The content of the letters was so damaging to the British government that Benjamin Franklin was dismissed as colonial Postmaster General and had to endure an hour-long censure from British Solicitor General Alexander Wedder-burn. (Murray, 2013)

Franklin was an Englishman turned rebel, and the British government swiftly replaced him as Postmaster General and therefore censor-in-chief. This was a very early example of the control over international communications within the Empire that was to be perfected in the "Victorian internet" telegraph era. At time of war, their approach to telegraph was simple: no encrypted telegraph traffic would be retransmitted by British operators. The comparison to the current interception of both plain and encrypted communications on the post-Victorian internet by both the British and U.S. governments and corporations is plain to see.

Conclusion: The Industrial-Surveillance Complex, Whistle Blowers and Governance

The world has changed less than we think, and the battle between tyranny and freedom is eternal and geographical. While the reach of international human rights law was severely limited in the nineteenth century, largely a matter of humanitarian aspects of the law of war and the extraterritorial application of domestic anti-slavery laws by the hyper-power Great Britain, we now live in what are claimed to be more enlightened times. The first internet link outside North America was to Norway (as part of the North Atlantic Treaty Alliance) in 1973. Four decades later, we have wired Africa, if a little less speedily than the Victorians. The cabling of the planet for the internet uses much the same undersea lanes and develops from those technologies. Geography matters, and so does territorial sovereignty. Information flows through those cables, and he who controls the cables controls the information.

The tapping of telegraph lines and blocking of encrypted messages was *de rigeur* in the Victorian era but has been challenged under international human rights law in the twenty-first century. On September 24, 2013, Brazilian President Roussef chastised President Obama at the General Assembly, and called for five fundamental digital rights on the internet:

(1) Freedom of expression, privacy of the individual and respect for human rights.
(2) Open, multilateral and democratic governance, carried out with transparency by stimulating collective creativity and the participation of society, Governments, and the private sector.
(3) Universality that ensures the social and human development and the construction of inclusive and non-discriminatory societies.
(4) Cultural diversity, without the imposition of beliefs, customs and values.
(5) Neutrality of the network, guided only by technical and ethical criteria, rendering it inadmissible to restrict it for political, commercial, religious or any other purposes.

The likelihood that multistakeholder civil society is able to exercise useful scrutiny and control over hyper-power politicians and their corporate partners may appear remote, and the call for international norms for human rights law quixotic, but the recent Brazil Internet Governance Summit is a real attempt to do so (Marsden, 2013). It could mark what some might call a tectonic shift in governance of communications, somewhat confirmed by the decision to reduce the US Department of Commerce's role in controlling the Domain Name System, reforms proposed on March 14, 2014, a month before that politically sensitive Brazil summit.[14] Cables may girdle the Earth in only 66.8 light milliseconds (rather than Shakespeare's forty minutes[15]), but we are more slowly emerging from a nightmare of covert internet surveillance into the shadowy half-light of governance of the corporations and surveillance agencies that have for so long controlled our information.

Notes

[1]   See illustrations and history at http://www.bletchleypark.org.uk/content/machines.rhtm
[2]   Foreign Minister Patino Aroca of Ecuador addressed the Security Council on August 6, stating: "We saw the size and the discretional nature of a massive surveillance apparatus that suddenly brought all the inhabitants of the planet closer than ever to an Orwellian nightmare. We now know that everyone is considered a usual suspect by U.S.A." At the same session, Foreign Minister Antonio de Aguiar Patriota of Brazil stated that:

"[I]nterception of communications and acts of espionage … violate sovereignty, harm relations between nations and constitute a violation of human rights, in particular to privacy and of our citizens to information."

[3]   Earle (2004) explains in detail that the "British Navy" itself was an extraordinary multinational collection of rogues and vagabonds (many "press-ganged" in port), most of them dumped unceremoniously when disabled in action or when peace broke out. The largest share of the men-o'-war available were actually privateers—voluntary warships out to make a quick buck by raising the colours and boarding their otherwise commercial rivals, to entirely legally overtake the ships and turn them into further privateers. The crews were either captured and ransomed, or if less valuable massacred or turned into mercenaries for the Crown.

[4]   Simon de Bolivar (attributed) 1829: "[The U.S.] appears destined by Providence to plague America with miseries in the name of Freedom" (Bushnell & Langley, 2008, p. 135).

[5]   Arthur Wellesley learnt his warrior trade at his brother's side in southern India in the last decade of the nineteenth century. The British were inspired by their very own 9/11: the "Black Hole of Calcutta," an incident in which British soldiers and other European civilians were entombed for the night of June 20, 1756 in a prison that led to between 40 and 123 dying of asphyxiation and complications. The British were to thrash the interior of Africa into submission after a later *cause celebre*, that of General Gordon who was killed at Khartoum in 1888, over a century later. It led to Barack Obama's Kenyan grandfather struggling for independence from this foreign occupation, and being tortured for his troubles in the 1950s.

[6]   The anti-pirate force off Somalia's coast in the early nineteenth century was made up of British privateers and enforcers against Arab slaver dhows (Earle, 2004). The special forces were men such as John Hanning Speke and especially Sir Richard Francis Burton (Farwell, 1990). The mercenaries were any number of men, including those in the Jameson Raid in South Africa which predicated the Boar War of 1899–1902.

[7]   The abolition of slavery in 1807 was inconvenient for West Indian sugar plantation owners, although they (including oligarch heir David Cameron's forefathers) were handsomely compensated. The writing was partly on the wall after the independence struggle of Haiti in 1803, in any case. Nelson was the notable sailor-hero in the West Indies in the 1790s who saved the plantation owners from French domination, and whose heroic death at Trafalgar cemented Britannia's ruling of the waves for what became the next century. It was far more inconvenient for the former colonies, who maintained their slavery-founded cotton plantations and needed fresh blood supplies from West Africa. By the 1820s, the newly victorious British Navy was in the mood to show American slavers who was boss of the Atlantic, and the extraterritorial extension of British moral economics was to remove the slave trading supply by the 1830s in the Atlantic, and by the 1860s in the Indian Ocean.

[8]   Brunel had created an extraordinary railway in the west of England, constructing the world's fastest form of locomotion (the 'Iron Duke' class locomotive achieved a record 80mph in 1845, only surpassed in speed in 1893) leaving from the world's largest building by area enclosed (the present Paddington Railway Terminus opened in 1854). The Flying Dutchman journey from London to Penzance (the final rail station before the transatlantic telegraph and now internet cable heads into the Atlantic Ocean) is today little faster than in the 1860s leaving from Brunel's great Terminus. From London to Exeter takes 3 hours 15 minutes on the fastest express in 2013, when the *Flying Dutchman* journey to Exeter took 4 hours 30 minutes in 1849: http://en.wikipedia.org/wiki/Flying_Dutchman_(train).

[9]   "Porth Kernow" in the native Cornish language.

[10]   See *R (on the application of) Cityhook Ltd & another* v *Office of Fair Trading* [2009], EWHC 57 (Admin) Case No: CO/7886/2006, at http://www.bailii.org/ew/cases/EWHC/

Admin/2009/57.html appealed from *Cityhook Limited v Office of Fair Trading* [2007] CAT 18 (03 April 2007) at: http://www.bailii.org/uk/cases/CAT/2007/18.html

[11] Prices for these cables' "landing rights" are extraordinarily high, and in the control of the Duchy-telecommunications companies' pleas for more reasonable prices rejected by the English courts as *ultra vires* the Crown prerogative. Not since King Arthur's legend has a prince extracted such a ransom for ownership of a Cornish beach. Today's cable companies discussed the Duchy's control as an existential territorial threat: "The real danger is that our industry must plot its own destiny and once we have accepted a covert proposal of this sought on Duchy beaches then it may quickly spread to other beach landings." In a bitterly contested ruling, the U.K. competition authority closed a decade-long investigation into the Duchy's monopolistic price gouging of U.K. and U.S. telecoms and submarine cable companies ('United Kingdom Cable Protection Committee'). Supra n. 10 at paragraph 31 per Level 3.

[12] By many separate contesting inventors, Morse in the U.S. for instance.

[13] The line had to be long and strong enough (2300 miles and 9000 tonnes) to be capable of surviving being paid out from a ship with engines mighty enough to power such an unholy leviathan that could smash through Atlantic hurricanes at a steady speed, never pausing in the face of the 100-foot waves that are common in that maelstrom (though in fairness cable laying was conducted in July–August). That enormous ship would have to be steady in storms to prevent breakage as it unspooled and laid the cable in the great Atlantic storms, and was the creation of Brunel's remarkable genius: the 700-foot long *SS Great Eastern* (launched in 1858 as *SS Leviathan*, only surpassed in size in the twentieth century).

[14] Details remain limited at time of writing, but the idea is that the Internet Assigned Numbers Authority (IANA) functions be further devolved to Internet Corporation for Assigned Names and Numbers (ICANN) by 2015. See National Telecommunications Infrastructure Administration (2014).

[15] The often used (in this essay) quotation "I'll put a girdle about the Earth in 40 minutes" is taken from Puck's exit in Shakespeare, W. (1590/1596) *A Midsummer Night's Dream*, Act 2, Scene 1.

References

Barty-King, H. (1980). *Girdle round the Earth: History of "Cable and Wireless"*. London: William Heinemann.

Bushnell, D., & Langley, L.D. (2008). *Simón Bolívar: Essays on the life and legacy of the liberator*. Rowman & Littlefield Publishing Group, Lanham Maryland.

Clarke, A.C. (1958). *I'll put a girdle round the Earth in forty minutes*. New York: American Heritage.

Earle, P. (2004). *The pirate wars: Pirates vs. the legitimate navies of the world*. London: Methuen.

EurActiv. (2013, July 3). *Parliament to launch enquiry into U.S. eavesdropping*. Retrieved from http://www.euractiv.com/justice/meps-set-inquiry-group-wiretappi-news-529048#.UdPo76hNdhI.twitter

Farwell, B. (1990). *Burton: A biography of Sir Richard Francis Burton* 1st ed, reprint, London: Penguin.

Glover, B. (2011). "The evolution of Cable & Wireless, part 2." *History of the Atlantic Cable & Undersea communications: From the first submarine cable of 1850 to the worldwide fiber optic network*. Retrieved from http://www.atlantic-cable.com/CableCos/CandW/Eastern/

Gustin, S. (2013, July 3). NSA scandal: As tech giants fight back, phone firms stay mum. Retrieved from http://business.time.com/2013/07/03/nsa-scandal-as-tech-giants-fight-back-phone-firms-stay-mum/#ixzz2Y1NVwnAN

Hills, J. (2007). *Telecommunications and empire*. Champaign, IL: University of Illinois Press.

James, L. (1998). *Raj: The making and unmaking of British India*. London: Little, Brown.

Kennedy, P.M. (1971). Imperial Cable communications and strategy, 1870–1914. *The English Historical Review, 86*, 728–752.

Khazan, O. (2013, July 16). The creepy, long-standing practice of undersea cable tapping. *The Atlantic*. Retrieved from http://m.theatlantic.com/international/archive/2013/07/the-creepy-longstanding-practice-of-undersea-cable-tapping/277855/

Kimberlin, D.E. (1994). Subject: Re: Need date of first undersea cable. *Telecoms Digest, 14*(7). Archived at http://massis.lcs.mit.edu/archives/history/underseas.cables

Kurbalija, J. (2013, October 7). *Back to cable geo-politics?* Retrieved from http://www.diplomacy.edu/blog/back-cable-geo-politics-first-part

Marsden, C. (2004). *Hyperglobalized individuals: The internet, globalization, freedom and terrorism*. 6 Foresight 3 at 128–140.

Marsden, C. (2013). *The road from Bali to Rio to dystopia*. London School of Economics Media Policy Blog, Internet Governance Series [Web log message]. Retrieved from http://blogs.lse.ac.uk/mediapolicyproject/2013/10/31/internet-governance-series-the-road-from-bali-to-rio-to-dystopia/#more-5543

Moglen, E. (2013, October 9). *Snowden and the future part I: Westward the course of empire*. Retrieved from http://snowdenandthefuture.info/PartI.html

Muchlinski, P. (2007). *Multinational enterprises and the law* (2nd ed.). Oxford: Oxford University Press.

Murray, C. (2013, October 11). *Edward Snowden gets Sam Adams award*. Retrieved from http://www.craigmurray.org.uk/archives/2013/10/edward-snowden-gets-sam-adams-award/

National Telecommunications Infrastructure Administration. (2014, March 14). NTIA announces intent to transition key internet domain name functions. Retrieved from http://www.ntia.doc.gov/press-release/2014/ntia-announces-intent-transition-key-internet-domain-name-functions

R (on the application of) Cityhook Ltd & another v *Office of Fair Trading* [2009], EWHC 57 (Admin) Case No: CO/7886/2006. Retrieved from http://www.bailii.org/ew/cases/EWHC/Admin/2009/57.html

Sampson, A. (1973). *The sovereign state: The secret history of ITT*. London: Hodder and Stoughton.

Shakespeare, W. (1590/1596). *A midsummer night's dream*, Act 2, Scene 1. Retrieved from http://shakespeare.mit.edu/midsummer/full.html

Standage, T. (1999). *The Victorian internet*. London: Phoenix Books.

The Return of Ideology and the Future of Chinese Internet Policy

Guobin Yang

After China's new leader Xi Jinping took office in November 2012, an ideological tendency with a Maoist imprint has become more visible in policy-making. This tendency is not a simple revival of Maoist practices, but a re-appropriation suited to new political goals. In the near future, internet governance in China is likely to combine Mao-style mass campaigns with the mobilization of law and civil society to proactively mold online expression and behavior.

When Xi Jinping officially became the new leader of the Chinese Communist Party in November 2012, observers anxiously looked for signs of political and media openings and reforms. Developments in 2013 show, however, that China's internet policy will likely remain unchanged. Indeed, whatever changes may happen will be toward more proactive and multi-pronged forms of management and control. In addition to the familiar methods of keyword filtering, blocking of websites, and monitoring and harassment of dissidents, the multi-pronged forms include using law to punish misdemeanors, using covert methods to monitor and channel online expression, and resorting to political campaigns to mold online expression and behavior. Beneath and beyond all these forms, I will argue, is an increasingly visible ideological thread vying to give coherence to an expanding system of internet control.

In less than two years after Xi assumed office, his leadership style has already betrayed an ideological element reminiscent of the Maoist period. Called "more Maoist than reformer" by the *Los Angeles Times* (Demick, 2013), Xi has reportedly revived the Maoist practice of self-criticism as a method of curbing corruption among party officials (Roberts, 2013). Maoist political practices such as the "mass line" have been brought back to official discourse, while the notion of civil society came under attack in the summer of 2013 as a Western import that does not fit Chinese reality (Huang, 2013). Xi's promotion of the idea of a Chinese dream, especially the use of the language of a great national rejuvenation after a century of national shame and humiliation, is in the lineage of an earlier Maoist language of anti-imperialism and national independence.

Xi's Maoist ideological slant is not a simple revival of Mao-era practices, but a re-appropriation suited to the new political goal of realizing a "Chinese dream." Now a signature concept associated with Xi Jinping, the idea of a Chinese dream was spelled out by Xi in a speech he gave on November 29, 2012, just two weeks after he became China's new president and Communist Party general-secretary. In that speech, he stated that while every Chinese has his or her own ideals and dreams, the greatest dream of all Chinese in modern history is the rejuvenation of the Chinese nation (Xinhua, 2012). The idea of a Chinese dream is smart. Because dreams are in one's mind, it provides ample room for individuals to give play to their own imagination. Thus even as the idea of a Chinese dream shares the strong national characteristic of the Mao era, it differs from the totalizing ideology of class struggle and revolution in that earlier time.

Second, the re-appropriation entails the incorporation of new elements suited to the new goal, as well as the reinvention of old elements. Campaign-style mobilization for policy promotion and implementation is an old method (Cell, 1977), but it is now revamped with the appeal of new media technologies. State-led campaigns are now carried out not only in newspapers and on television but increasingly on the internet and through social media. A central new element is the notion of soft power introduced from Western social science discourse. The establishment of Confucius Institutes around the globe and the promotion of the global influences of Chinese media agencies are among the more notable examples of this soft power approach (Zhang, 2009). But perhaps most importantly, learning to speak the language of soft power means learning to speak a smarter language, one that takes into account the taste and linguistic habits of the audience and the reception context. Thus in a *People's Daily* article on October 10, 2013, Vice Minister of Propaganda Cai Mingzhao stresses "telling China's story well": "Whether or not China's story can be told well, and whether or not China's voice can be disseminated well, crucially requires us to look at whether or not audiences are willing to listen and able to understand, whether or not they can form positive interaction with us, and engender even more resonance" (Cai, 2013).

Multiple factors explain the Maoist ideological turn under Xi. First, it is not a radically new development but retains some degree of continuity with the practices under Xi's predecessor Hu Jintao, when references to Mao's theory of handling social contradictions were common in the official discourse about maintaining social stability (Trevaskes, 2013) and when a campaign to promote Maoist "red culture" was ablaze in the city of Chongqing (Yang, 2014).

Second, the system of "stability maintenance" instituted to contain social protest in the past decade has the ironic effect of causing more instability (Feng, 2013). The failure of that system to curtail social unrest and pacify an increasingly angry and grievous citizenry (Yang & Zheng, 2012) compels the new leadership to rethink its strategy to govern. Third, economic developments and international relations in recent years have fed the sentiments of popular nationalism in China. Nationalistic social movements, such as anti-Japanese protests over the disputes about the Diaoyu Islands, have taken place both on the internet and in the street. In public discourse, this popular nationalism often uses the nationalistic and anti-imperialist ideological discourses of the Mao era. Thus, the official re-appropriation of Maoist ideology has a popular basis. Moreover, as the son of a deceased high-ranking Chinese Communist Party leader and a member of the first age-cohort socialized under the new socialist regime, Xi's personal background and youthful experience attuned him to the power of ideology in shaping human behavior.

Finally, resorting to ideological influence is consistent with the tradition of cultural governance in China, a tradition that reaches deep into Chinese political culture, from imperial Confucian rituals to the earlier history of the Chinese Communist Party (Perry, 2013). It is also based on a new, Foucauldian understanding about the nature and technologies of power and governance. The gradual overhaul of China's administrative institutions over the years is informed by ideas from the disciplines of public administration and public management (Pieke, 2012). Social control, including the control of the internet, is no longer seen as a simple technical or policing issue. Instead, it requires a systemic approach, part of which is the ideological shaping of the citizenry. As Pieke (2012, p. 150) puts it, "Ideology is an indispensable aspect in the creation of regime support, no longer intending to generate 'belief' in the party, but to cultivate responsible, trusting, and 'high-quality' citizens who inhabit an active, autonomous, and governable society."

The ideological thread in Xi's policy approach inevitably tinges China's internet policy. The crackdown on "internet rumors" in the summer of 2013 is a case in point. On August 23, 2013, an internet celebrity qua venture capitalist Xue Manzi was detained in Beijing on charges of soliciting prostitution (Barboza, 2013). A naturalized American citizen, Xue was an active and critical commentator on current affairs on the popular microblog platform Sina Weibo. Chinese internet users, often called *netizens*, speculated that the real reason for his detention was his critical and influential voice on Weibo. Making an example of him was a warning to other influential figures to restrain their online expression.

Such speculation was not unfounded. Soon afterwards, on September 8, 2013, the Chinese Supreme People's Court and Supreme People's Procuratorate issued a judicial interpretation, stating that people who post false information on the internet may face up to three years in prison if the posting is viewed more than 5,000 times or retweeted 500 times (Kaiman, 2013a). This new rule was applied on September 20, 2013, when a 16-year-old boy in a small town in the remote Gansu province was detained for posting a message on Weibo, which had indeed been retweeted more than 500 times (Kaiman, 2013b). He was charged with posting false information that led to a street demonstration and disrupted social order.

Although the hapless lad was later released under public pressure, no doubt was left about the aggressiveness of the new campaign against internet expression, when, about three weeks after his detention, Xue Manzi was shown on China's major television news channels repenting about his misdemeanor. He confessed on camera that as a popular blogger with 12 million followers on Weibo, he felt like an emperor. He apologized for posting unverified information and misguiding his followers (Wan, 2013). It became clear that Xue Manzi was a selected target in a national campaign to sanitize internet expression.

In October 2013, the story about a thriving new occupation called "internet opinion analyst" attracted international attention. This is a job to monitor and analyze online expressions for "harmful" contents. Government agencies hire internet opinion analysts to monitor online information considered harmful to their image. Business firms hire them to track online comments on their products. Both government and business agencies may resort to monetary or other means to have negative information removed from the web.

In the near future, while the current practices of internet filtering, blocking, and censoring continue, more efforts may be expended by the Chinese government on channeling and containing internet expression through ideological work and cultural governance more broadly (Perry, 2013). Internet opinion analysis will prove to be a profitable business as it is used by more and more government agencies and business firms to monitor political or commercial behavior among citizens and consumers. Consistent with the official rhetoric of resuscitating the "mass line" from the tradition of the Chinese Communist Party (Buckley, 2013), internet control will likely rely more on societal efforts, including the mobilization of civil society organizations and internet firms, as well as the promotion of self-discipline for internet businesses and individual internet users (Yang, 2013). Popular platforms such as Sina Weibo already maintain "community committees" of social and cultural elites to help monitor postings on the website and enforce community rules. Finally, more efforts may be expected to go into expanding official websites, encouraging government agencies to take up social media, and telling smarter stories about the internet to the Chinese people and the world. In short, the multi-pronged forms of internet governance in China will put more emphasis on winning the hearts and minds of the people and generating bankable stories in the global marketplace of internet narratives.

References

Barboza, D. (2013, August 25). Chinese-American Commentator and Investor Is Arrested in Beijing. *The New York Times*. Retrieved from http://www.nytimes.com/2013/08/26/world/asia/chinese-american-commentator-and-investor-is-arrested-in-beijing.html?_r=0

Buckley, C. (2013, August 19). China takes aim at Western ideas. *The New York Times*. Retrieved from http://www.nytimes.com/2013/08/20/world/asia/chinas-new-leadership-takes-hard-line-in-secret-memo.html?_r=0

Cai, M. (2013, October 10). Tell China's story well, spread China's voice well [in Chinese]. *People's Daily*. Retrieved from http://politics.people.com.cn/n/2013/1010/c1001-23144775.html?utm_source=The+Sinocism+China+Newsletter&utm_campaign=c994565df6-Sinocism10_10_131&utm_medium=email&utm_term=0_171f237867-c994565df6-24571569. Translated by Rogiers Creemer at http://chinacopyrightandmedia.wordpress.com/2013/10/10/chinas-foreign-propaganda-chief-outlines-external-communication-priorities/

Cell, C.P. (1977). *Revolution at work: Mobilization campaigns in China.* New York, NY: Academic Press.

Demick, B. (2013, June 8). China's Xi more Maoist than reformer thus far. *Los Angeles Times.* Retrieved from http://articles.latimes.com/2013/jun/08/world/la-fg-china-xi-20130608

Feng, C. (2013). The dilemma of stability preservation in China. *Journal of Current Chinese Affairs, 42*(2), 3–19.

Huang, C. (2013, July 20). Leading leftist academic mocked over 'Maoist' op-ed. *South China Morning Post.* Retrieved from http://www.scmp.com/news/china/article/1286519/leading-leftist-academic-mocked-over-maoist-op-ed

Kaiman, J. (2013a, September 10). China cracks down on social media with threat of jail for "online rumours." *The Guardian.* Retrieved from http://www.theguardian.com/world/2013/sep/10/china-social-media-jail-rumours

Kaiman, J. (2013b, September 20). China detains teenager over web post amid social media crackdown. *The Guardian.* Retrieved from http://www.theguardian.com/world/2013/sep/20/china-detains-teenage-web-post-crackdown

Perry, E.J. (2013). Cultural governance in contemporary China: "Re-orienting" party propaganda. Harvard-Yenching Institute Working Paper Series, 2013.

Pieke, F.N. (2012). The Communist Party and social management in China. *China Information, 26,* 149–165. doi:10.1177/0920203X12442864

Roberts, D. (2013, October 3). Xi Jinping is no fun. *Business Week.* Retrieved from http://www.businessweek.com/articles/2013-10-03/china-president-xi-jinping-revives-self-criticism-sessions-in-maoism-lite

Trevaskes, S. (2013). Rationalising stability preservation through Mao's not so invisible hand. *Journal of Current Chinese Affairs, 42*(2), 51–77.

Wan, W. (2013, September 15). China broadcasts confession of Chinese-American blogger. *Washington Post.* Retrieved from http://www.washingtonpost.com/world/china-broadcasts-confession-of-chinese-american-blogger/2013/09/15/3f2d82da-1e1a-11e3-8459-657e0c72fec8_story.html

Xinhua. (2012, November 29). Xi Jinping: Inherit the past, open up the future, continue to forge ahead toward the goal of a great Chinese national renaissance. Retrieved from http://news.xinhuanet.com/politics/2012-11/29/c_113852724.htm

Yang, G. (2013). Social dynamics in the revolution of China's internet content control regime. In M. Price, S. Verhulst, & L. Morgan (Eds.), *Routledge Handbook of Media Law* (pp. 285–302). London: Routledge.

Yang, G. (2014). Mao quotations in factional battles and their afterlives: episodes from Chongqing. In A. Cook (Ed.), *Mao's little red book: A global history* (61–75). Cambridge: Cambridge University Press.

Yang, L., & Zheng, Y. (2012). Fenqings (angry youth) in contemporary China. *Journal of Contemporary China, 21*(76), 637–653. doi:10.1080/10670564.2012.666834

Zhang, X. (2009). China as an emerging soft power: Winning hearts and minds through communicating with foreign publics? *Global Media Journal, 4,* 1–14.

The US Digital Divide: A Call for a New Philosophy

Sharon Strover

The digital divide has become embroiled in discussions about technologies that range well beyond those earliest circumstances related to computer access and use, where the term first cropped up. Caught between a public discourse that espouses equality in opportunity as well as the tremendous bounty at the end of the technological rainbow and another that celebrates a marketplace distribution of technologies and services, US policy around the digital divide has waffled between unsystematic efforts to provide access to technology and to cultivate technological capabilities, and a trenchant affirmation in the ability of the market to provide the best array and distribution of technological resources.

The digital divide has become embroiled in discussions about technologies that range well beyond those earliest circumstances related to computer access and use, where the term first cropped up. Caught between a public discourse that espouses equality in opportunity as well as the tremendous bounty at the end of the technological rainbow and another that celebrates a marketplace distribution of technologies and services, U.S. policy around the digital divide has waffled between unsystematic efforts to provide access to technology and to cultivate technological capabilities, and a trenchant affirmation in the ability of the market to provide the best array and distribution of technological resources. We can do better.

Policymakers and scholars started talking about the digital divide when personal computers made their way into households in the 1990s, a timeline that included a growing internet and the World Wide Web. While a cadre of people in Washington trumpeted the significance of the internet and moved forward on National Information Infrastructure deliberations and pronouncements, scholars and critics grew increasingly alarmed at disparities in using computers across certain populations. The usual populations were scrutinized—women, members of minority groups, and the elderly—and the National Telecommunications and Information Administration (NTIA) initiated the first of many surveys (that continue to this day with the Census Bureau) beginning with its *Falling through the net* studies in 1995. Its early surveys documented the acquisition of computers and their use in home, work, and school settings, and investigated the demographic factors that predicted ownership and use, and in so doing they helped to define the digital divide as a matter of *physical access* to the technology.[1] And, yes, women, minorities and the elderly, and more generally the poor and the less educated, were indeed using computers less often. With these studies, the prescriptive or aspirational role of computers and internet use, the idea that one would need these skills and technologies in order to function within the information society, entered the mainstream.

From a policy standpoint, the notion also was linked to the idea of universal service, the language found in telecommunications regulation that advocates rural and urban parity—in its original version, comparable telephone service and comparable rates—in an affirmation of a social contract that Schement (2009, p. 3) called "the trinity of opportunity, participation and prosperity." When the 1996 Telecommunications Act crafted its Schools and Libraries program (often called e-rate) as part of its universal service provisions, it was a tacit recognition that public institutions had significant roles in providing access to important "advanced telecommunications and information services" and that the FCC should shepherd federal investment in equipping those institutions with computers and internet connections (Telecommunications Act of 1996, Section 254). E-rate fund eligibility is indexed by rural location and economic disadvantage, essentially providing more support for schools and libraries that presumably have less access to resources. E-rate became the most tangible federal commitment to remedying the digital divide, defining it as an economic and geographical issue, and its focus was clearly on technology as the solution.

To their credit, some states, municipalities, and community organizations mobilized to try to remediate access to computers, and, later, access to the internet. Wrapped in the language of combatting the digital divide, these efforts have ranged from investing in school-based computers and internet connections, to designing and launching training programs in computer literacy, to expanding physical locations—so-called third places—where people could use computers and have internet access. A few states such as Texas prioritized rural and remote locations for their funding, providing discounted high speed connections to regions that limped along with sub-par telecommunications infrastructure (Texas Public Utility Regulatory Act, 1995).[2] California initiated several different programs and also invested in studies and data-gathering that examined the digital divide across its geographical regions and population groups. Other states have had similar programs over the past 15 years. In the aggregate, they represent considerable investment, but also share limited demonstration of success, few formal evaluations, and limited integration with any relevant federal programs.[3] The overall effect was scattershot, uncoordinated, and largely devoid of research that could demonstrate the utility of various investments.

The access definition of the digital divide underscores a "drive by" approach to remediating the digital divide: simply insure that computers and connections are available, and the rest will take care of itself. As Warschauer (2002) wrote, "issues of content, language, education, literacy, or community and social resources" were not part of the discourse. Rather, it was the access definition that figured in aid programs: get technology into the hands of the demographic groups identified in the surveys as on "the wrong side" of the divide, and the problem will be resolved.

That definition broadened in the 21st century. By the year 2000, NTIA's writing about the digital divide emphasized both *how* people were accessing "digital tools," and the *purposes* motivating their use, signaling a new facet of the divide: the idea that capabilities and training figured into the divide questioned the notion that technology alone was a sufficient remedy. However, shortly thereafter under the Bush Administration, the phrase digital divide itself morphed into *digital inclusion*: declaring the war won, in the Bush Administration subsequent federal efforts and statements emphasized the strides the market had made in eliminating technological inequalities (NTIA, 2002).[4]

Against the backdrop of new policy positioning the marketplace as the means to achieve digital inclusion, a broad and enthusiastic campaign lauded the potential of the internet for the economy. The dot.com boom of the late 1990s and early 2000s was in full swing, and technology based optimism proliferated. Internationally, countries vied with each other to establish "Information Age" or "Information Economy" or "Digital Economy" plans, generally focused on technology investments as vehicles for broad social and economic makeovers. Even the dot.com bust in the early 21st century did not dissolve enthusiasm about the centrality of computers and internet for economic progress and belief in the market's ability to deliver their benefits. When former FCC Commissioner Michael Powell was asked about his plans to attack the digital divide it is not surprising that his answer was "You know, I think there's a Mercedes divide. I'd like to have one. I can't afford one" (C-Span, 2001), essentially suggesting that certain populations' inabilities to access or use computers or the Internet were their fault: the market discriminates across all products, so why single out computer or internet services? While perhaps best remembered for that line, Powell expanded on his point by stating the essential conundrum that faces government when questioned about its role in innovation processes: When can one justify government intervention? What's the difference between market failure and market discrimination?

The alternative view to marketplace solutions swings between espousing stopgap measures and addressing large scale economic inequality. Certainly the Obama Administration's efforts to structure stimulus programs to improve broadband access fall into the first camp (American Recovery and Reinvestment Act of 2009 or ARRA). By (1) extending infrastructure to rural regions that lacked high quality broadband, (2) delivering training to urban core populations that lacked computer and internet literacy, and (3) providing middle mile facilities that could reduce costs to last mile providers and thus enable them to offer more affordable broadband, the NTIA and Department of Agriculture stimulus projects that were funded at $7.2 billion contributed modest additions to extant network resources and were a slight nod in the direction of assisting people who lack computer and internet skills.[5] And it was, after all, only a two year program.[6]

Some scholars acknowledge that the gaps in technology use and access are among many factors that keep certain population groups at a disadvantage. Broader matters of economic inequality go hand-in-hand with disadvantages in using computers and the internet, and our policymaking around the digital divide has fallen far short of acknowledging the roles of entrenched poverty and mechanisms of inequality that contribute to the situation. Addressing large scale social inequalities seems far beyond the reach of contemporary communication policy making. However, in the face of the bigger problems of social inequality, some digital divide-related efforts can at least "help to show the way out" (Servon, 2002, p. 2) even if they cannot touch the fundamental sources of inequity. So what do we know about the divide now, and about the policies that can create meaningful change?

We know quite a bit about the locations of the digital divide. One product of the ARRAprograms was improved data gathering around network capabilities and locations, and consequently we have better—though not perfect—maps illustrating where basic network infrastructure does not reach. Specific rural areas, for example, can be targeted for infrastructure support. We know that many rural areas lack broadband connections that meet the 4 Mbps downstream speed threshold, and that the access and connection quality issues are more significant to rural populations than to urban.[7] When it comes to higher speeds, rural areas are far behind their urban counterparts: NTIA reports that while 88% of urban areas have access to speeds of 25 Mbps, only 41% of rural areas are comparable. About one-third of the population on tribal lands lack access. This means that infrastructure funds should target rural regions. It also suggests that government support programs (such as those in the FCC's Connect America program, the successor program to one facet of universal service, the High Cost Fund) should prioritize rural areas and communities that do not meet speed thresholds.

We also know a great deal about the impediments to using computers and the internet that go beyond access. Roughly 98% of Americans *can* obtain access to some type of high speed connection at either their home, work, or at a nearby public place, but a much lower 69% actually subscribe to it at home. What keeps about 30% of the country away from high speed services at home? Lower incomes and less education are associated with not owning computers or using the internet or broadband. Households with children and younger households also are more likely to adopt computers and broadband services. Internet and computer usability and relevance also have emerged as significant factors associated with non-adoption (Hargittai & Hinnant, 2008; van Dijk, 2003; van Deursen & van Dijk, 2011; Mossberger, Tolbert, & Stansbury, 2003; Mansell, 2002; Gangadharan & Byrum, 2012). The original access divide has evolved into one defined by skills and "meaningful use."[8] Demographic factors interact with the perceived relevance of Internet content as well as its affordability.

Where should policy focus beyond basic network access? First, the least known and least controllable factor in the equation is the price of internet access. There are no national datasets gathering this information, and surveys indicate it is a major predictor of internet use (along with perceived usefulness of the internet). Gathering systematic data on price would be a first step toward understanding how providers and policy and users can work together to structure an affordable access and use scenario. The price data that does exist strongly suggests that people in the U.S. pay more for lower quality broadband service than is typical in many other industrialized countries (Crawford, 2013; FCC, 2012a);[9] we also know that prices seem to be lower in the locations where competitive ISP services exist.

Even if regulating service prices is out of the question, understanding how price influences the value equation for users would be an important step, as would experimenting with providers around alternative price points and working with users on financial assistance possibilities. One policy solution may be to encourage alternative ISP structures, such as municipally provided services, that are less motivated by profit in their operations. While approximately 20 states have laws that forbid or limit municipal provision of broadband services, revisiting this policy and creating ways to maximize such alternative structures may create a viable structure to address price issues, with additional possible benefits in terms of community based training and support that might logically accompany a locally controlled infrastructure.

A second and related point concerns the role of conventional service providers such as cable and phone companies in remedying digital inequalities. Long used to offering commercial services that people simply could accept or reject, providers have been slow to address the challenges presented by the low income households that desire broadband service. The FCC's latest Lifeline experiments, in which providers come up with strategies to appeal to these households and in exchange receive federal funding, represent an interesting behavioral economics approach to encouraging adoption (FCC, 2012b). Other incentive programs should be developed to bring the providers into the arena. The related problem of encouraging commercial providers to build the high capacity fiber networks that other areas of the world enjoy is related to the broader issue of how the government might intervene in cultivating and distributing necessary digital resources.

Third, while communication policy cannot overhaul social structure, it can make inroads in educating people regarding using computers and the Internet. In the current decade, online interactions have moved well beyond the prescriptive status that characterized them in the 1990s: access to online resources or information is now normative, taken for granted by an ever larger array of basic commercial and other service providers, including government services. This means everyone needs at least minimal capability to access and use the internet. Recent NTIA-sponsored programs elicited some understanding of best practices for training (NTIA, 2013);[10] a long history of similar efforts from libraries around the country also provides guidance. Arguably, a long range view to resolve the divide would recognize libraries are primary sites for providing both access and training and assistance: although sometimes beleaguered by budget cuts, libraries exist in both small and large towns, and have done an admirable job in helping people to use the internet. That role should be supported financially.

This raises a fourth point related to educating and training users who currently lack internet skills. Many non-profits were involved in the stimulus-funded grants from either federal or state (or even local) sources to establish public computing centers and training programs. However, the duration of such funding is frequently short; the last round of federal grants from NTIA, for example, lasted only two years. Long-standing, community-based non-profits doing this work need grants that extend for much longer periods of time. Indeed, it probably would have been much better policy to have had longer grants at reduced annual funding so that the NGOs themselves are stable and can plan ahead. The feast-or-famine method of living from grant to grant is not socially beneficial; the non-profits contributing to resolving the divide could use something more methodical. A serious digital divide literacy effort would stabilize funding, evaluate the best providers of services, and make long term investments.

Finally, consider the role of mobile communications in the digital divide. While some say ubiquitous mobile phones means everyone can access the internet, there are reasons to question what mobile internet might mean for the digital divide. Mobile phones are widely popular through the country, among rich and poor, educated and less educated. However, while higher income households maintain cell phone subscriptions in addition to some sort of fixed broadband access, statistics demonstrate that lower income households increasingly are using the mobile phone for their internet access, probably in lieu of a home-based broadband service.[11] This presents some problems.

Cell phone-based internet access has obvious limitations for tasks such as applying for jobs or even searching for complicated information; the screen size impedes full functionality. As the next generation of wireless devices with larger screens becomes available, and as the speeds on wireless networks improve, this may become moot. However, the cost factors with smartphone-based internet access are still formidable for low income individuals, as are usability issues—are smartphone-only internet users able to execute the same sorts of tasks that are typical of fixed broadband users? As more bandwidth-intensive applications evolve, and if services continue to charge by speed tiers, we are once again facing the prospect of another type of digital divide, one in which higher income households afford high speed mobile services and lower income households are left with less capable services; rural areas likely will be the last in line for the best wireless service.

The quality disparity has not kept some from suggesting that the costliest, rural households—the "last" 250,000 households for which wireline infrastructure would cost $14 billion—should in fact use less expensive wireless services and forego the "luxury" of a fiber or cable-based broadband service. This pragmatic consideration brings us back to the original question: how do cost and "business case" aspects of owning and using computers and the internet trade off with equity concerns? When do opportunity costs and the penalties of being technologically marginalized reach a point that requires intervention? This is ultimately a question of political values and political will.

This review shows that while access and use of computer and internet-related technology have grown steadily, so too a divide persists that stratifies people in different spatial (urban–rural), age, and socio-economic groups. As internet-related capabilities are increasingly embedded in routine aspects of life in the U.S. and elsewhere, inabilities to either access or make use of the tools that mainstream society takes for granted will once again penalize and marginalize population groups. Most of our policy mechanisms consistently sidestep the inequalities that usually accompany the introduction and use of new technologies. Even though we have had some policy interventions attempting to explore or remedy the digital divide, to date they remain mired in a philosophy that still advocates for very limited interventions and a strong belief that the market will ultimately resolve such issues. Our episodic policy approaches to problems of internet and computer availability as well as use and ability issues have been neither consistent nor long-term in vision. This calls for revising our view of the digital divide toward a perspective that acknowledges the *continuous* challenges of new technologies and inequalities and that proactively considers approaches to enhancing both supply (provider) solutions while also cultivating an understanding of user challenges and possibilities.

Notes

[1]   For example, NTIA's (1995) report explores the relationship between computer ownership and use and sex, income, race and ethnicity, age, location (rural/metro), age and other demographic variables.

[2]   Texas' Telecommunications Infrastructure Fund created through the Texas Public Utility Regulatory Act of 1995 provided approximately $1.5 billion dollars to schools, libraries, and other facilities for computers and internet access from 1995 to 2003.

[3]   For example, the Departments of Agriculture and Education have had many programs focused on enhancing telecommunications infrastructure and equipping schools for internet access, but there is scant evidence that states have linked or leveraged their efforts with federal investments. NTIA's Technology Opportunities Program, which ran from 1994 to 2004, provided approximately 300 grants (valued at about $0.5 billion when matching funds are factored) to state and local governments, tribal groups, schools and libraries, and other community based organizations for digital network technology demonstration projects. Modest evaluation efforts were funded, but there is no evidence that their findings led to any policy changes or improved efforts to remediate the digital divide.

[4]   For example, NTIA's *A Nation Online* (2002) reports the gains of the past decade, and states that the growing market for technologies and services was adequately providing for the diffusion of these technologies and the internet itself.

[5]   NTIA's programs (the Broadband Opportunities Program) funded middle mile facilities, sustainable broadband adoption training programs, and the establishment or upgrading of several public computing centers; the Rural Utilities Service ARRA program (Broadband Initiatives Program or BIP) contributed to extending broadband networks into rural unserved or underserved regions.

[6]   Indeed, the premise of dramatically scaling up training and digital literacy programs over a two-year timeframe, and then halting all funding, does a huge disservice to the infrastructure of the largely non-profit programs that rose to the task of implementing

local training, got their programs running, and then laid off all the staff they had hired and trained, all within the two-year time frame of the Recovery Act. The duration of the ARRA funding itself was clearly temporary.

[7]   Indeed, the FCC reports that fewer than half of U.S. households have a fixed internet connection meeting their standard (FCC, 2013). About 19 million households lack access to fixed broadband networks, and of those, over 14 million are in rural regions.

[8]   This is a very deliberate reference to this concept's development in the U.S. health field.

[9]   The FCC also reports in 2012 that the U.S. prices for fixed broadband are in the "middle" of those found in a 38 country survey, but higher in higher-speed ranges (FCC, 2012a).

[10]   NTIA released its Broadband Adoption Toolkit in 2013.

[11]   A 2013 Pew Internet and American Life survey showed the people whose internet access is generally through their cell phones are less educated, non-White, with lower incomes, and younger (Pew Research Internet Project, 2013).

References

American Recovery and Reinvestment Act of 2009, Pub. L. 111-5.

Crawford, S. (2013). *Captive audience: The telecom industry and monopoly power in the new gilded age*. New Haven, CT: Yale University Press.

C-Span. (2001). New FCC Chairman meet and greet. Originally broadcast on C-Span, February 6. Retrieved from http://www.c-span.org/video/?162428-1/new-fcc-chairman-meet-greet

FCC. (2012a, August). *Eighth broadband progress report*. Retrieved from http://www.fcc.gov/reports/eighth-broadband-progress-report.

FCC. (2012b). *In the matter of Lifeline and Link Up Reform and Modernization, WC Docket No. 11–42*. Retrieved from http://www.fcc.gov/document/14-projects-chosen-lifeline-broadband-pilot-program-competition

FCC. (2013). *Internet access services*. Retrieved from http://hraunfoss.fcc.gov/edocs_public/attachmatch/DOC-324884A1.pdf

Gangadharan, S., & Byrum, G. (2012). Introduction: Defining and measuring meaningful broadband adoption. *International Journal of Communication, 6*, 2601–2608.

Hargittai, E., & Hinnant. A. (2008). Digital inequality. *Communication Research, 35*, 602–621. doi:10.1177/0093650208321782

Mansell, R. (2002). From digital divides to digital entitlements in knowledge societies. *Current Sociology, 50*, 407–426. doi:10.1177/0011392102050003007

Mossberger, K., Tolbert, C., & Stansbury, M. (2003). *Virtual inequality: Beyond the digital divide*. Washington, DC: Georgetown University Press.

National Telecommunications and Information Administration [NTIA]. (1995). *Falling through the net: A survey of have-nots in rural and urban America*. Retrieved from http://www.ntia.doc.gov/ntiahome/fallingthru.html

National Telecommunications and Information Administration [NTIA]. (2002). *A nation online: How Americans are expanding their use of the internet*. Retrieved from http://www.ntia.doc.gov/legacy/ntiahome/dn/anationonline2.pdf

National Telecommunications and Information Administration [NTIA]. (2013). *Broadband adoption toolkit*. Retrieved from http://www2.ntia.doc.gov/files/toolkit_042913.pdf

Pew Research Internet Project. (2013). *Cell internet use 2013*. Retrieved from http://www.pewinternet.org/2013/09/16/main-findings-2/

Schement, J. (2009). Broadband, internet and universal service. In A. Schejter (Ed.), *... and communications for all* (pp. 3–37). New York: Lexington Books.

Servon, L. (2002). *Bridging the digital divide: Community, technology and public policy*. Malden, MA: Blackwell.

Telecommunications Act of 1996, Public Law No. 104-104, 110 Stat. 56 (1996).

Texas Public Utility Regulatory Act of May 12, 1995, 74th Leg., R.S. Ch. 231, 1995 Tex. Gen. Laws 2017.

Van Deursen, A., & van Dijk, J. (2011). Internet skills and the digital divide. *New Media & Society*, *13*, 893–911. doi:10.1177/1461444810386774

Van Dijk, J. (2003). The digital divide as a complex and dynamic phenomenon. *The Information Society*, *19*, 315–326. doi:10.1080/01972240309487

Warschauer, M. (2002). Reconceptualizing the digital divide. *First Monday*. Retrieved from http://firstmonday.org/htbin/cgiwrap/bin/ojs/index.php/fm/article/viewArticle/967/888

Crypto War II

Sascha D. Meinrath & Sean Vitka

Revelations about the National Security Agency (NSA) and other intelligence agencies' widespread surveillance in the summer of 2013 have accelerated America's path toward a second critical battle over public cryptography. Because so much more of our society is now online, Crypto War II will be a far more devastating conflagration than the Crypto War of the 1990s—one that pits our fundamental right to control the computers and smart devices that are becoming an everyday part of our lives against a combination of corporate and government interests. While the Summer of Snowden has received widespread media coverage, the potential alignment of private and public sector surveillance interests pose a far greater threat to free communication in the 21st century than we've yet realized.

Revelations about the NSA and other intelligence agencies' widespread surveillance in the summer of 2013 have accelerated America's path toward a second critical battle over public cryptography. Because so much more of our society is now online, Crypto War II will be a far more devastating conflagration than the Crypto War of the 1990s—one that pits our fundamental right to control the computers and smart devices that are becoming an everyday part of our lives against a combination of corporate and government interests. While the Summer of Snowden has received widespread media coverage, the potential alignment of private and public sector surveillance interests pose a far greater threat to free communication in the 21st century than we've yet realized.

The Situation Today

In a world where surveillance capabilities are increasingly baked into the fabric of the internet's architecture, end-to-end encryption is a last line of defense. The knowledge that everyone's data is susceptible to sweeping government surveillance is pushing more people, companies, and organizations to use additional measures to secure their information (Robinson, 2013). But these measures may soon become the casualty of bad policymaking and over-exuberant law enforcement mandates. Internet service providers are increasingly focused on prioritizing certain internet traffic and degrading specific services and applications (Brodkin, 2014). Previously, open internet rules stopped providers from degrading peer-to-peer traffic, but those rules were thrown out in 2014 when the D.C. Circuit Court of Appeals ruled against the Federal Communications Commission (FCC) (Zajac & Shields, 2014). The court found that the FCC had failed to "promulgate net neutrality regulations ... under the proper legal framework." Without net neutrality, network monitoring and discriminatory behavior by ISPs is certain to increase.

Encrypting data (and obfuscating what type of application or service is being used), makes discrimination far more difficult, but such practice also draws the ire of surveillance agencies and their defenders. Such groups treat personal encryption as a target and sometimes go so far as to depict opponents of surveillance as anti-social agitators (Brooks, 2013). In the first Crypto War, the government wanted to prevent the widespread use of strong encryption—for all intents and purposes, classifying math as a munition and clamping down on the export of cryptographic software. When outright bans failed, the government attempted to mandate that back doors be implemented in cryptographic products (the Clipper Chip battle) and, finally, that a third party keep backdoor keys "in escrow" in case the government needed them. The argument was familiar: law enforcement felt it needed to be able to access communications to ensure public safety and national security. Even today, the NSA views the use of encryption as a targetable offense (Goodin, 2013). While the government eventually lost Crypto War I, the Snowden files document a massive, secret conspiracy to undermine strong encryption by introducing back doors into numerous hardware and software products that has persisted since that defeat (Simonite, 2013).

Aligned Interests

Unlike Crypto War I, however, today there is also unprecedented corporate interest in data collection and surveillance. One particularly problematic industry practice is the move by ISPs to create tiered or preferential service offerings. Plans to create tiered services have been floated for years—enabled in part by constant pressure toward less competition in the broadband market. In fact, within mobile broadband services, tiering of various applications (e.g. voice, texting, data) are already normative. But if an ISP can't tell what sort of application is being used, it doesn't know whether to prioritize or deprioritize a specific communications stream—which is why good encryption breaks one of the fundamental assumptions for this new business model. Since encryption can help circumvent discriminatory practices, the incentive to use it will expand with practices like tiering.

ISPs could use various mechanisms to dissuade users from encryption. Terms of service could even go so far as to deprioritize or forbid encrypted traffic—forcing users to trade privacy for speed. Internet service providers already stigmatize and discriminate against other protocols and services. It was only a few short years ago that Comcast blocked BitTorrent, claiming (without merit, as was proven once the practice was stopped) that this was necessary to prevent network congestion.

In a post-Snowden world, encryption services will likely become a growing percentage of network traffic. As the debate over application discrimination continues, a growing number of users report experiencing a precipitous and unexplained drop in quality of bandwidth-heavy services like Netflix (Fitzgerald & Ramachandran, 2014). Such service degradation indicates discrimination on the user-side, data exchange deals (or lack thereof) on the provider end, or both. In response, a number of consumers have already begun to take matters into their own hands—for instance, by routing traffic through Virtual Private Networks.

Meanwhile, corporations like Google have begun encrypting the data transferred among its data centers and with its users to prevent government snooping. Thanks to their immense political power, these corporate responses to government surveillance have provided some of the most—and arguably, one of the only—effective avenues to stop the slide toward a second Crypto War. But while we may see momentary "wins," it's likely that there will be a private sector split with ISPs and content providers facing off on opposite sides of the encryption battle lines.

Such battles are likely to migrate to one of the most powerful, and least prepared, venues for technological debate on the planet—the U.S. Congress. Within this arena, law enforcement's influence is more powerful. The consistent argument is that encryption and anonymity endanger society (Clapper, 2013). With this new corporate interest, industry lobbyists will simultaneously argue that encryption is undermining their intellectual property and other business interests, and that users freely accept surveillance via the purchase of their products and use of their applications. Their narrative regarding consumer discontent is that unhappy users could always "vote with their feet" and switch providers.

Ever-Increasing Surveillance

As consumers become more privacy-conscious, it remains an open question just how this combination of corporate and government interests will respond. The U.S. government has long required many service providers in America to install surveillance capabilities within their IT infrastructures and applications. The Communications Assistance for Law Enforcement Act mandates that certain digital services be able to comply with wiretap orders, a legally enforced security vulnerability. Such demands draw anonymity oriented services, like Lavabit, into the national security agencies' crosshairs. Their data is not only sought pursuant to statutory tools like CALEA, but also through secret contracts, national security letters, and even outright hacking by government employees (Walters, 2013). The U.S. government has utilized other tactics as well, creating and endorsing encryption standards designed around subtle, difficult-to-diagnose, exploits that are later utilized in surveillance activities (Schneier, 2005). This is the primary reason why conflicting reports over whether the NSA knew or exploited the Heartbleed vulnerability have caused grave alarm among cryptography experts.

For years, many analysts have expected CALEA "reform," a euphemism for expansion of the act's surveillance mandates. This expansion, which law enforcement has long pushed for, could bring new services under CALEA's umbrella, while also creating severe financial penalties for those companies that do not comply. Under such a regime, if a business were to provide encrypted peer-to-peer communication after such reform, like many services that have gained significant popularity since 2013's surveillance revelations, they would likely also need to provide law enforcement with a mechanism to intercept and decrypt them (Savage, 2010). Security expert Bruce Schneier describes the government's ambitions concisely: "What the FBI wants is the ability to eavesdrop on everything" (Schneier, 2013).

Corporate-governmental collaboration in surveillance (via CALEA and other mandates) is itself a business. As *The Washington Post* reported in August 2013, the NSA paid $394 million into the Corporate Partner Access Project in 2011, and expected to spend another $278 million in 2013 (Timberg & Gellman, 2013). Today, an option that is being floated to modify current surveillance practices would have private entities act as the surveillance data-keepers instead of the NSA—with, of course, a significant payout of tax dollars to these storage proxies.

These surveillance efforts have inspired a dramatic increase in the array of services and applications that are encrypted end-to-end (Hern, 2013). This response from privacy oriented constituencies is a response to both data discrimination and government surveillance—and also indicates that we are entering a new online era epitomized by a growing data-obfuscation arms race. Left unchecked, the relevant surveillance mechanisms will shift from network-based to device-based. That is, one can imagine a CALEA II that creates mandates that devices themselves integrate mechanisms that enable surveillance. In essence, the hardware and software integrated into our smart cars and homes—and even our bodies themselves—will be legally required to be insecure, to the financial benefit of parties seeking to control our communications.

Conclusion

The above series of events would portend frightening political pressure on lawmakers. It is difficult to imagine a politician standing up for privacy and free speech rights when opposition of this position, from both well-moneyed private industry and law enforcement, proclaim that encryption supports 'copyright infringement, child pornography, and terrorism'—all at once. This is the Crypto War II narrative.

However politically dire the current situation is, we can take heart that the key success from the first Crypto War has, in fact, withstood the test of time. Individuals everywhere can and do use tools like Pretty Good Privacy to encrypt their e-mail and other communications whenever and wherever they are. If one wishes to secure a laptop, phone, or other communication device, encryption like PGP can make it exceedingly difficult to undermine the integrity of communications. The nearly 20 years that strong encryption has been publicly available has not led the world into disarray, nor have terrorists and criminals taken over. In fact, strong encryption has been singularly important for a variety of critical economic and political endeavors (Stecklow, Sonne, & Bradley, 2011). The online world as we know it simply would not exist without strong encryption—everything from credit card purchases to securing the passwords on our favorite social media website requires it.

Crypto War I was a long-fought affair, and eventually the forces of free speech won. But Crypto War II will be a far more grueling slog pitting privacy and free speech aficionados against both governmental and corporate interests. Losing Crypto War II would be disastrous—creating unprecedented collateral damage, dangerous precedents, and potentially game-changing implications that would fundamentally undermine participatory democracy—in particular, the free speech on which it depends—on a global scale. There are, however, several concrete actions that we can take to prevent us from heading down this trajectory. Three key tactics are discussed below.

First, ensure that the locus of control over communications is in the hands of end users and within edge devices. Today's mass surveillance is predicated upon centralized mechanisms for collecting data that are located in the core of our communications networks. But so long as we can use strong encryption and anonymizing technologies, we can still be fairly certain that our communications are secure. While we've won the right to use strong encryption, the next battles will be over who controls our edge devices—and losing now would undermine everything we won in the first Crypto War.

Second, we must enshrine Internet Freedom and open internet rules and ensure that discriminatory practices do not become the new norm. End users are perfectly capable of deciding when they want to prioritize streaming video or an outgoing upload. Today, a legal battle is raging inside the Beltway about how the Federal Communications Commission will oversee the internet—and it is up to the FCC to disrupt the data obfuscation arms race that is certain to occur if ISPs begin to prioritize and degrade services.

Third, reiterate that the right to privacy is sacrosanct and includes the right to use strong encryption, steganographic communications, and anonymizing technologies. Anonymity has been a foundational part of U.S. culture, from Publius, the pseudonym used by some Founding Fathers when publishing the Federalist Papers, to anonymous comments in online forums. It is essential to free speech and a free society.

Taken together, these reforms would change a trajectory that is rapidly hurling us toward Crypto War II and help ensure that Democracy in the 21st century remains true to the inalienable rights it is predicated upon. To accomplish this peace, we need to overcome both entrenched business interests as well as the ever-prevalent fear of the unknown. Our privacy and free speech rights will not survive if we lose these coming battles—and with this corporate-government alignment against encryption, the fight will be harder than ever before.

References

Brodkin, J. (2014, February 21). Netflix packets being dropped every day because Verizon wants more money. *Ars Technica*. Retrieved from http://arstechnica.com/information-technology/2014/02/netflix-packets-being-dropped-every-day-because-verizon-wants-more-money/

Brooks, D. (2013, June 10). The solitary leaker. *The New York Times*. Retrieved from http://www.nytimes.com/2013/06/11/opinion/brooks-the-solitary-leaker.html

Clapper, J.R. Office of the Director of National Intelligence. (2013). DNI statement: Why the intelligence community seeks to understand online communication tools & technologies. *IC on the Record*. Retrieved from http://icontherecord.tumblr.com/post/58838654347/welcome-to-ic-on-the-record

Fitzgerald, D., & Ramachandran, S. (2014, February 18). Netflix-traffic feud leads to video slowdown. *The Wall Street Journal*. Retrieved from http://online.wsj.com/news/articles/SB10001424052702304899704579391223249896550

Goodin, D. (2013, June 20). Use of Tor and e-mail crypto could increase chances that NSA keeps your data. *Ars Technica*. Retrieved from http://arstechnica.com/tech-policy/2013/06/use-of-tor-and-e-mail-crypto-could-increase-chances-that-nsa-keeps-your-data/

Hern, A. (2013, December 31). Email is broken—but Dark Mail Alliance is aiming to fix it. *The Guardian*. Retrieved from http://www.theguardian.com/technology/2013/dec/31/email-broken-dark-mail-alliance-fix-silent-sircle-snowden

Robinson, F. (2013, August 8). U.S. surveillance programs spur EU efforts to tighten data protection rules. *The Wall Street Journal*. Retrieved from http://online.wsj.com/news/articles/SB10001424127887324522504579000702411343532

Savage, C. (2010, September 27). U.S. tries to make it easier to wiretap the internet. *The New York Times*. Retrieved from http://www.nytimes.com/2010/09/27/us/27wiretap.html

Schneier, B. (2005, February 18). Cryptanalysis of sha-1. *Schneier on Security*. Retrieved from http://www.schneier.com/blog/archives/2005/02/cryptanalysis_o.html

Schneier, B. (2013, June 4). The problems with CALEA-II. *Schneier on Security*. Retrieved from https://www.schneier.com/blog/archives/2013/06/the_problems_wi_3.html

Simonite, T. (2013, October 8). NSA's own hardware backdoors may still be a "problem from hell." *MIT Technology Review*. Retrieved from http://www.technologyreview.com/news/519661/nsas-own-hardware-backdoors-may-still-be-a-problem-from-hell/

Stecklow, S., Sonne, P., & Bradley, M. (2011, June 1). Mideast uses Western tools to battle the Skype rebellion. *The Wall Street Journal*. Retrieved from http://online.wsj.com/news/articles/SB10001424052702304520804576345970862420038

Timberg, C., & Gellman, B. (2013, August 29). NSA paying U.S. companies for access to communications networks. *The Washington Post*. Retrieved from http://www.washingtonpost.com/world/national-security/nsa-paying-us-companies-for-access-to-communications-networks/2013/08/29/5641a4b6-10c2-11e3-bdf6-e4fc677d94a1_story.html

Walters, J. (2013, December 29). NSA "hacking unit" infiltrates computers around the world—report. *The Guardian*. Retrieved from http://www.theguardian.com/world/2013/dec/29/der-spiegel-nsa-hacking-unit-tao

Zajac, A., & Shields, T. (2014, January 14). Verizon wins net neutrality court ruling against FCC. *Bloomberg*. Retrieved from http://www.bloomberg.com/news/2014-01-14/verizon-wins-net-neutrality-court-ruling-against-fcc.html

Persistent Pursuit of Personal Information: A Historical Perspective on Digital Advertising Strategies

Inger L. Stole

While much about digital advertising appears revolutionary, it would be wrong to accept the notion that customer surveillance is a modern phenomenon. Although the internet's technological advances have taken advertising in new directions and the practice of "data-mining" to almost incomprehensible extremes, nearly all of what is transpiring reflects some of the basic methods developed by marketers beginning a hundred years ago. In this essay, I argue that the emerging nature of digital advertising has important consequences for how scholars think about internet policy issues as well as how media scholars think about the changing relationship of advertising to content production.

When Edward Snowden revealed in 2013 that the National Security Agency (NSA) was secretly monitoring internet users, the news almost instantly ignited public awareness and alarm about the ubiquitous nature of digital surveillance. People were particularly shocked to learn that the NSA worked closely and harmoniously with nearly all of the major internet corporations—ranging from AT&T and Verizon to Google and Microsoft—to track the entirety of Americans' digital activities. The exposé debunked the conventional wisdom of the internet as a place where users enjoyed privacy and control over their online activities, a mythology that had largely been true in the 1990s.

Contrary to common belief, the driving force behind the internet's transition from a place where users were anonymous and in charge to one where individuals were constantly monitored by powerful unaccountable interests was not national security, it was commercialism. Initially, the internet was commonly viewed as a "democratizer of information," a medium that was capable of breaking the codependent relationship between advertisers and mass media that had been the norm since the early 20th century (McChesney, 2013). As a result, the advertising industry was highly concerned. Procter & Gamble CEO Edwin Artz had the "chilling thought" that "emerging technologies were giving people the opportunity to escape from advertising's grasp altogether." He argued that corporations needed to "grab all this new technology in our teeth once again and turn it into a bonanza for advertising" (Turow, 2012, pp. 40–41). Exactly how this could be accomplished was the subject of considerable debate, especially because early internet users rejected banner and pop-up ads, and relished the notion of cyberspace as a noncommercial sphere.

By the end of the 1990s, companies such as Yahoo! and later Google and Facebook began to realize that information about internet users had significant commercial value for advertising and for direct sales, which were increasingly merging. Systems and protocols were introduced and refined to make it possible to surreptitiously track people's activities online. The business model was simple: "If people get something for free on the Internet, they are not the customer, they are the product." Most important, emerging "smart advertising" could be targeted to individuals wherever they went on the internet and on their mobile phones. It was no longer necessary to waste money on ads that went to people who had no interest in the product being advertised. Advertisers no longer needed to subsidize journalism or media content production. Thus, over the past two decades, the internet has become commercialized to an astonishing extent. As it has morphed into a dominant institution, the advertising industry has been a key ally.

While much about digital advertising appears revolutionary, it would be wrong to accept the notion of customer surveillance as a modern phenomenon. Although the internet's technological advances have taken advertising in new directions and the practice of "data-mining" to almost incomprehensible extremes, nearly all of what is transpiring reflects some of the basic methods developed by marketers beginning a hundred years ago. At the same time, the emergence of digital advertising has important consequences for how scholars think about internet policy issues, as well as how media scholars think about the changing relationship of advertising to content production.

The starting point for any analysis is to recognize that modern advertising is a function of corporate capitalism. By the 20th century, most large firms operated in oligopolistic markets that eschewed explicit price competition. The giant firms competed, but not through what was derided as "price warfare." Advertising became a crucial way to distinguish between so-called "parity" products: largely interchangeable products being sold at the same price. The content of ads had little to do with actual or important product attributes, focusing instead on evocative themes that might capture consumers' attention. As we look at the specific manner in which the internet has developed in the United States, we can see that it has far less to do with technology than it does with the pressures associated with modern corporate capitalism, with advertising as Exhibit A.

Although advertising is a function of corporate capitalism, the nature of the institution is determined to a significant extent by regulation and policies. That is as true today as it was a century ago. For a generation of consumer advocates from the 1920s to the 1940s, advertising was an absurd institution more likely to propagandize consumers than to give them useful product information (Stole, 2006, 2012). As the 1920s came to an end, consumers had become increasingly aware of the problems associated with brand advertising and galvanized accordingly. An increasingly vocal consumer movement led by Consumers' Research, and later Consumers Union, exposed fraud and manipulation by American manufacturers and argued that advertising was not providing consumers with sufficient product information. According to critics, advertising played on people's insecurities by "guiding" consumers through the task of choosing the "right" products. They objected to being told that bad breath, old-fashioned furnishings, or smoking the wrong brand of cigarettes could hinder their professional and social success, and they pointed to the high premium put on branded, as opposed to generic, consumer products.

Most of all, the burgeoning consumer movement was concerned that the advertising industry's lack of accountability to the public hindered the proliferation of free and competitive markets. This set the stage for a five-year legislative battle over advertising regulation, including several congressional hearings and several revised versions of a federal bill. Ultimately, due to a set of well-developed public relations and lobbying strategies and considerable influence over the commercial mass media, the advertising industry won the fight. The Wheeler-Lea Amendment to the Federal Trade Commission Act—ostensibly "reform legislation"—was passed in 1938, but for the most part it recognized and legitimized the status quo in advertising practices.

There was a resurgence of aggressive consumer activism in the 1960s and 1970s—which worked, among other things, to remove cigarette advertising from television—but such movements tend to flounder in eras when the rule of capital is unquestioned and unquestionable in the political culture. In view of the seemingly endless economic stagnation, the U.S. may be entering an era when a significant number of Americans will no longer regard corporations and the capitalist system as sacred institutions. If that is the case, the nature of digital commercialism will likely become an area of political attention and debate.

The surreptitious collection of data on consumers to make it possible for advertisers to better manipulate them is not a product of the internet; it is deeply embedded in the very nature of modern advertising. In the early part of the 19th century, under the guise of providing an added service, manufacturers invited consumers to request product samples, booklets, and recipes. Also, in exchange for repeat purchases of a particular brand, consumers were rewarded with premiums and prizes, including trading cards, wall hangings, games, calendars, and collectible tokens. In 1905, loyal buyers of Larkin soap could choose from 116 different premiums in exchange for their saved labels, ranging from soaps, jellies, coffee, and teas to perfumes. Thirteen years later, those who had saved up enough soap wrappers could use the company's premiums to outfit an entire household (including a piano).

To mostly unsuspecting consumers, the exchange of personal information for promotional products might have appeared to be a quid pro quo, but unbeknownst to the average person, manufacturers used the personal and geographical information they obtained for demographic targeting of new and existing consumers. While obviously unsophisticated by today's standards, the practice of using trusted information about consumers for marketing research had been established (Strasser, 2004).

When compared with present-day mining of consumer data, such practices might appear benign, but they underscore the extent to which advertisers monitored consumers and tracked their behaviors outside the point of purchase. Most often, advertisers obscured the full extent of their marketing strategies, making consumers think the "gift" they received represented the longest end of the stick.

The 1930s debate over advertising regulation had revealed a deep public distrust of advertising, and nothing, including industry claims about its usefulness to society, even to the sustainability of a free press, did much to satisfy the public. Public awareness that product advertising was more persuasive than informative had affected its credibility as a sales tool. But while discussions of advertising regulation had revealed some rather unflattering facts about the industry and its methods, the ongoing practice of monitoring consumers' behavior without true disclosure was never part of this debate. Few, except for a limited number of advertising practitioners, know how important the mining of marketing data on the unsuspecting public was for its continued success. Thus, as America entered the post-World War II era, when national prosperity, even military security, hinged on corporate growth, additional strategies to boost sales were desperately needed.

The practice of collecting data about consumers' habits and preferences accelerated in the 1950s, when advertisers embraced the use of psychological methods to improve their marketing techniques. Assisted by "motivational research," the industry was determined to mine the public subconscious and soothe "discovered" fears and longings with appropriate consumer products. Much of this research was conducted on unsuspecting individuals (including children) who were never told the true purpose of the various studies. Simultaneously, the industry worked diligently at collecting demographic data about individuals in attempts to create consumer profiles (based on income, education, and social status) so that potential buyers could be more precisely targeted for marketing purposes (Packard, 2007).

Although motivational research in and of itself enjoyed a rather short heyday, the advertising industry continued to work on perfecting its strategies. By the late 1960s, consumer cynicism toward advertising reached a new high, and the 1970s excitement over recording devices that allowed TV ads to be bypassed had the advertising industry on edge. The backlash came through extensive use of product placements. Increasingly sophisticated in their targeting, advertisers knew what people watched and how to reach them. In light of this game of "cat and mouse," in which consumers try to hide from advertising while advertisers keep devising new strategies to "trap" them, it is easy to understand why the initial vision of the internet as a commercial-free medium would appeal to the public. It is also easy to understand why this notion would represent a severe headache for the industry. In the end, not only did advertisers persevere; they succeeded in turning the internet into a tool for consumer surveillance—a strategy so successful that it was embraced by national security and military agencies.

Well aware that direct advertising appeals often failed to resonate with an increasingly cynical public, a century ago the advertising industry was quick to create a strategy of blurring the distinction between advertising and content in the printed press. The introduction of commercial radio not only advanced this practice, it helped perfect the industry's early data-mining strategies. Most shows were owned and produced by advertisers, who monitored the demographic makeup of their listening audiences by offering free promotional products of various kinds. Among the many programming formats, the radio serial offered one of the best vehicles for gathering marketing information. The fictional characters on the programs would incorporate the advertiser's products into the story line and "befriend" the listening audience, giving listeners the impression that the show reflected the trials and tribulations of actual people. Urged by advertisers to provide personal information in exchange for product samples and photos of cast members, unsuspecting listeners provided free marketing data that could be used and possibly sold (Lavin, 1995). The practice came to a temporary halt in the late 1950s when the broadcasting networks succeeded in wresting programming control from advertisers, but it re-emerged as soon as advertisers gained control of the internet and turned the collection of user information into the main currency.

Today more than ever, advertisers need to have their messages received and embraced by their target audiences. The commercially driven internet model heightens the blurring of advertising and media content and obscures distinctions between producers and consumers of news, entertainment, and advertising. Much to the advertising industry's delight, internet users have become an integral part of the marketing mix. Adding to the industry's enthusiasm is the fact that so many of us are trapped within this "matrix," making it difficult to offer a critical perspective on the situation. Still, as scholarly debates about the internet's role continue, it might be useful to consider the historical strategies that informed its commercial structure.

References

Lavin, M. (1995, June). Creating consumers in the 1930s: Irna Phillips and the radio soap opera. *Journal of Consumer Research, 22,* 75–89. doi:10.1086/209436

McChesney, R.W. (2013). *Digital disconnect: How capitalism is turning the internet against democracy.* New York, NY: New Press.

Packard, V. (2007). *The hidden persuaders.* Brooklyn, NY: IG.

Stole, I.L. (2006). *Advertising on trial: Consumer activism and corporate public relations in the 1930s.* Urbana: University of Illinois Press.

Stole, I.L. (2012). *Advertising at war: Business, consumers, and government in the 1940s.* Urbana: University of Illinois Press.

Strasser, S. (2004). *Satisfaction guaranteed: The making of the American mass market.* Washington, DC: Smithsonian Books.

Turow, J. (2012). *The daily you: How the new advertising industry is defining your identity and your worth.* New Haven, CT: Yale University Press.

The Media Policy Tower of Babble:
A Case for "Policy Literacy Pedagogy"

Becky Lentz

This essay argues that "media policy studies" are important enough to warrant more deliberate critical scholarly and curricular attention. Yet the complexity of media policy presents many challenges. One response is ramping up situated learning apprenticeship opportunities that offer newcomers to the field much-needed experience in what this essay argues is the critical "genre-work" of public-interest oriented policy advocacy practice. In addition, civil society organizations hosting apprentices as interns or fellows help to populate a feeder system into a field that is woefully undernourished. This essay also calls for media policy education parallel to that enjoyed in higher education by other policy fields such as environmental, public health and human rights studies.

The public is besieged with warnings about the incapacity of "the media," broadly conceived, to fulfill their democratic potential. In response, many media policy scholars informed by democratic or social movement theory place their hopes on digital activism or reviving journalism as a defense against the surveillance society and information insecurity. Studies are mostly actor-centered, featuring vitally important legions of anonymous hackers or media activists. At the same time, public intellectuals are working to reform intellectual property norms while open source advocates and digital dissidents sidestep policy roadblocks by producing commons-like alternative media platforms. Media scholars warn against further media consolidation and concentration, whilst digital rights and internet freedom advocates demand greater civil society involvement in the decisions of states, multinational bodies, and corporations. Last but not least, an expanding international community of internet governance scholars argues for more accountable and transparent multistakeholder approaches that involve civil society, not just governments and corporations (Bennett, 2010; Bollier, 2009; Castells, 2012; Coleman, 2013; Dean, Anderson, & Lovink, 2013; DeNardis & Raymond, 2013; MacKinnon, 2013; McChesney, 2013; Scott, 2014).

Traditional public sphere theory, that is, the Habermasian normative framework, argues that the best defense against threats to democratic media is an informed public adequately equipped for rational public debate. To be sure, there are many critics of the Habermasian framework, but donor institutions and philanthropists determined to salvage journalism or promote social media's promise do not appear to be among them. Shoring up journalism builds better content enterprises, be they public, private, or some combination of the two; however, it does not build the movement infrastructures needed for sustainable policy advocacy in the public interest. If university faculty hiring and course offerings are another indicator of priorities, there is much respect for all-things-digital: digital journalism, digital culture, digital humanities, and digital media education. Yet despite its importance to the future of democracy, we see scant attention to "digital media policy" or even "policy literacy." Being called upon to participate in episodic media policy struggles, to sign petitions, contribute to issue campaigns, re-Tweet arguments, watch mesmerizing TED Talks, or take part in protests at opportune flashpoints does not an educated digital citizen make. What *does* are opportunities to participate in the situated practices of experienced media policy advocates. How else to populate and sustain a public interest advocacy sector similar to that in policy fields such as environmental protection and human rights? The challenge to those trying to create such educational experiences is the interdisciplinary breadth and depth of this policy field, which encompasses broadcasting, telecommunications, internet, and information policy, not to mention a good bit of political science, economics, computer engineering, and legal expertise. The diversity of issues traveling under the umbrella term "media policy" contributes to an incoherence that actually undermines policy pedagogy. Although the students in my media governance course take many other media-related courses, each year they will remark, about 12 weeks into the term, "this is so important! Why haven't we heard about any of this before in any of our *other* classes?"

Definitional Problems

Braman's essays about the field's definitional problem are a case in point, as are the variety of encyclopedic entries and books on the topic (for example, see Napoli, 2008). In the U.S. context, for instance, Braman notes that after covering media policy's links to the Bill of Rights and the First Amendment, things get complicated quickly, especially after adding technology to the mix (Braman, 2004). In 21st century media policy scholarship, she argues, our focus is now more on the constitutive role in social and political life of content and distribution infrastructures. This author has argued that in the digital media environment, content and conduit are co-constitutive, thus equal attention must be given to issues of infrastructure alongside the political economy of content production, distribution, reception, and exchange (Lentz, 2010).

Braman illustrates this classificatory dilemma by describing how media policy embraces several related problems: technology-based convergence problems; practice-based problems; policy-based problems; and issue-based problems. She also points out a multitude of definitional perspectives used to map this field of inquiry, for instance, by topical area, legacy legal categories (e.g. statutory vs. regulatory), media industry type, stage of an information production chain (e.g. creation, processing, storage), or intended societal impact (e.g. protecting children from harmful content). She settles on a broad vision that accepts "a multiplicity of definitional faces, each of utility at a different stage of the policymaking process," recasting media policy as information policy: "all law and regulation that deals with information creation, processing, flows and use" (Braman, 2004, pp. 161–176).[1]

These and other well-intended definitional efforts contribute more, not less, to what I call the media policy tower of babble. Confusion and debate over terminology, entry points, and theoretical foci only obscure rather than clarify what one must know to intervene in policy areas like those mentioned earlier. This is not to suggest by analogy that arriving at an overarching definition of media policy is hubristic, but the fact remains that the sheer complexity of issues, institutions, aspirational goals, threats and concerns, legal doctrines, and technologies requiring mastery confounds efforts to design an education that equips graduates with the capacity to *produce* policy change.

Points of Entry for Media *Policy* Studies

As with communications studies, media policy studies are defined less by a canon of core texts than by their objects of study. Permeable intellectual boundaries demand rigorous interdisciplinary training, and some measure of practical experience. Media policy scholarship matters to democracy, freedom of information and expression, access to knowledge, economic and community development, cultural identity, and personal privacy. All offer a suitable vantage point for study. Communities of practice are an equally good entry, be they media producers, media audiences, cultural workers, consumer activists, communication rights advocates, journalists, open source developers, children's and women's right activists, or social justice activists. Or, it can be approached according to key concepts such as neoliberalism, democratic theory, public sphere theory, economic development, globalization, international development, or human rights. Finally, courts, legislatures, regulatory agencies, or international bodies are another entry point for study.

Media policy education interrogates history, legal doctrine and frameworks, institutions, and aspirational goals, but without direct experience, media policy remains relatively abstract, its impact being less visible than, say, pollution or the explicit violation of human rights. Exceptions of course, include infrequent but vitally important spikes in public awareness like the millions of signatures gathered during the media consolidation debate of 2003 (Moyers, 2003), the online protests during the SOPA/PIPA debates (Lentz, 2013), or the extensive media coverage of the NSA/PRISM affair that has made massive government surveillance an open secret.

Still, events such as spectrum auctions have considerable implications for national treasuries, but few lay people even know such marketplaces exist. Newcomers have to connect media policies to lived experience to understand what is at stake. Yet media policy scholars, practitioners, and public interest advocates speak the languages of many different disciplines. The overall project enjoys no coherent moniker like climate change or human rights. It is referred to as ICT policy, communication and information policy (CIP), communication law and policy, or internet governance; all encompass multiple, intersecting objects of study.

Teaching about the management, performance, design, and potentially nefarious uses of electronic media resources is a complex undertaking that requires deliberate attention to a robust media policy literacy agenda. We need to cultivate in university students a sense of citizenship beyond voting or conscientious consumption, and inculcate media policy literacy in the same way we do for environmental education in secondary, post-secondary, *and* adult education.

Media Literacy Should Include Critically-oriented Media *Policy* Literacy

Media *policy* literacy from a public interest perspective requires changing traditional notions of media literacy, which, critics observe, often mean merely "the ability to access, analyse, evaluate and communicate messages in a variety of forms" (Lunt & Livingstone, 2011, p. 122). Whilst media literacy agendas are now being expanded by governments to include *digital* media literacy, the overall focus remains, with a few exceptions, protectionist (Wallis & Buckingham, 2013):

> Media literacy here seems individualised, prioritising consumers and consumer choice over citizens and citizens' rights, and prioritising protection over participation. (Lunt & Livingstone, 2011, p. 125)[2]

Some argue that media literacy programs being advanced by government communication authorities actually serve deregulatory agendas. Livingstone and colleagues caution that "the more readily people are shown to have sufficient media literacy (if this can be specified), the more readily deregulation is legitimated" (p. 129).

Robust media *policy* literacy offers a potential counterweight to such a neoliberal media education agenda. Whereas digital media literacy may distract attention from deregulation, critical media policy literacy would develop capacity to intervene on deregulation or liberalization agendas. Yet to do so, critically minded media policy scholar advocates need to cultivate partnerships with public interest policy practitioners and advocates to create, and help to fund, opportunities for students to participate, at least peripherally, in communities of practice engaged in media policy work. Livingstone and colleagues assert, "the critical analysis of media literacy not as an inert skill or the property of an individual but rather as a social, contextualised capability" (p. 135). They cite Street's attention to social practices as forms of knowledge, which are always embedded in social practices, such as those of a particular job market or particular educational context and the effects of learning that particular literacy will be dependent on those particular contexts. (Street, 2003, pp. 77–81)

I would add that media policy literacy is a precondition for informed engagement in media policy struggles. For public interest advocates in particular, it is "necessary knowledge" for reforming or transforming media and communication systems for public, not just corporate, ends. While media education's goal may be to produce more effective or responsible ways of *using* media and technology, media *policy* pedagogy should engender the capacity to recognize and mobilize what Bitzer argues is "the rhetorical situation," or kairos: propitious moments for decision or action, in this case, in media policy struggles (Bitzer, 1992). Apprentices need to be able to navigate the temporal and discursive complexity of policy advocacy practice (Postill, 2013; Streeter, 2013) while doing genre-work alongside experts who are already part of a community of practice (see Bawarshi & Reiff, 2010, for discussion of the sociolinguistic concept of genre as a social practice and its links to knowledge-making). Media policy literacy emerges not just from the classroom or from scholarly writing, but directly from experience, something the media policy tower of babble with its multiplicity of approaches, entry points, and objects of study cannot facilitate unless it explicitly embraces practice. Media policy education must draw on a situated theory of learning in the sense advanced by Lave and Wenger (1991). It needs to include institutions, legal doctrines, aspirational goals, constituencies of interest, and specific policy issues like communication rights, freedom of expression, broadband inclusion. Internships, fellowships, exchange, or residency programs bring academic study to life.

Institutional Supports for Media Policy Literacy?

Despite media policy's clear political significance, there are too few academic programs preparing students to become professors of media policy or to represent the public interest in government, corporations, or media policy advocacy organizations. There are also too few civil society organizations, sustainable academic centers, institutes, or think tanks in media policymaking.

Why the media policy field remains so under-resourced confounds many working in this area. Donors that include the Ford Foundation, the Open Society Institute, and the Media Democracy Fund have already invested millions. So why is there still a mere handful of media policy courses in information schools, media and communication studies programs, and political science departments? Why not degrees or certificates in media policy? Why aren't more public affairs and public policy programs teaching media policy? Why aren't more programs looking beyond the study of journalism or faddish "new media" phenomena to address information, communication, and technology policy? Why are there still so few handbooks, encyclopedias, readers, and journals dedicated to media policy?

A point of entry might be to piggyback on the civic education agenda currently sweeping through higher education. In fact, several academic institutions and civil society organizations have been experimenting with programs to build media policy literacy as part of university education. Students in these programs get hands-on experience with expert media policy advocacy practitioners. Yet there are still too few of these programs, and little prepared curricular material or funding support for them, not to mention articles on reflexive pedagogy and related theory building (Lentz, 2014).

A media future that inspires and cultivates innovation, openness, and participation depends on the capacity of people to consider themselves as more than merely digital consumers. Critically minded media policy scholars have an obligation to team up with open source, media democracy, media justice, and freedom of expression communities of practice to render classrooms as collaboratories of theory and practice. Universities can also open their doors to advocates as "professors of practice," creating "sabbaticals for radicals" that allow scholars and students to learn from practitioners, and for practitioners to enjoy opportunities for reflection. University professors teaching media policy courses can also create educational consortia to share syllabi, with oral history projects as possible points of praxis that bring together teaching, research, and practice. Indeed, there are many opportunities to work through the media policy tower of babble that undermines advancing public engagement in one of the most important areas of policy studies of our time.

Acknowledgements

I would like to thank the anonymous reviewers of this article for their thoughtful comments and suggestions. Thanks as well to the Canadian Social Sciences and Humanities Research Council (SSHRC) and McGill University for their support of research related to ideas put forward in this article.

Notes

[1]   Braman offers an additional taxonomy of entry points for the study of Internet policy (Braman, 2012). Other recent definitional efforts can be found in D'Haenens, L., Mansell, R. & Sarikakis, K., Eds. (June 2010). Special Issue: Media Governance: New Policies for Changing Media Landscapes. Communication, Culture & Critique, Volume 3, Issue 2, pp. 131–223.

[2]   Livingstone cites a more recent UNESCO statement on media literacy as an example of an empowerment perspective: "Empowerment of people through information and media literacy is one important prerequisite for fostering equitable access to information and knowledge, and building inclusive knowledge societies. Information and media literacy enables people to interpret and make informed judgments as users of information and media, as well as 10 become skillful creators and producers of information and media messages in their own right" (p. 125).

References

Bawarshi, A.S., & Reiff, M.J. (2010). *Genre: An introduction to history, theory, research, and pedagogy*. Anderson, SC: The WAC Clearinghouse and Parlor Press LLC. Retrieved from http://wac.colostate.edu/books/bawarshi_reiff/

Bennett, C.J. (2010). *The privacy advocates: Resisting the spread of surveillance*. Cambridge, Massachusetts: MIT Press.

Bitzer, L.F. (1992). The rhetorical situation. *Philosophy & Rhetoric, 25*, 1–14. Retrieved from http://www.jstor.org/stable/40237697

Bollier, D. (2009). *Viral spiral: How the commoners built a digital republic of their own*. New York, NY: New Press. Retrieved from http://thenewpress.com/books/viral-spiral

Braman, S. (2004). Where has media policy gone? Defining the field in the twenty-first century. *Communication Law and Policy, 9*, 153–182. Retrieved from http://www.tandfonline.com/doi/abs/10.1207/s15326926clp0902_1

Braman, S. (2012). Internet policy. In M. Consalvo & C. Ess (Eds.), *The handbook of internet studies* (1st ed., pp. 137–167). Hoboken, NJ: Wiley-Blackwell.

Castells, M. (2012). *Networks of outrage and hope: Social movements in the internet age*. Cambridge: Polity.

Coleman, E.G. (2013). *Coding freedom: The ethics and aesthetics of hacking*. Princeton, NJ: Princeton University Press.

Dean, J., Anderson, J.W., & Lovink, G. (2013). *Reformatting politics: Information technology and global civil society*. London, UK: Routledge.

DeNardis, D.L., & Raymond, M. (2013). *Thinking clearly about multistakeholder internet governance* (SSRN Scholarly Paper No. ID 2354377). Rochester, NY: Social Science Research Network. Retrieved from http://papers.ssrn.com/abstract=2354377

Lave, J., & Wenger, E. (1991). *Situated learning: Legitimate peripheral participation* (1st ed.). Cambridge, UK: Cambridge University Press.

Lentz, B. (2013, September 27). Beneath the glitz of digital activism. *In the tank: A blog from the New America Foundation*. Retrieved from http://inthetank.newamerica.net/blog/2013/09/beneath-glitz-digital-activism

Lentz, B. (2014). Building the Pipeline of Media and Technology Policy Advocates: The Role of 'Situated Learning'. *Journal of Information Policy, 4*, 176–204.

Lentz, R.G. (2010, October 28). Media infrastructure policy and media activism. In J.D.H. Downing (Ed.), *Encyclopedia of social movement media* (pp. 323–236). Thousand Oaks, CA: Sage Publications, Inc.

Lunt, P., & Livingstone, S. (2011). *Media regulation: Governance and the Interests of citizens and consumers* (1st ed.). Thousand Oaks, CA: Sage Publications Ltd.

MacKinnon, R. (2013). *Consent of the networked: The world-wide struggle for internet freedom*. New York, NY: Basic Books.

McChesney, R.W. (2013). *Digital disconnect: How capitalism is turning the internet against democracy*. New York, NY: New Press.

Moyers, B. (2003, October 10). Bill Moyers on big media. *NOW*. Retrieved from http://www.pbs.org/now/commentary/moyers27.html#

Napoli, P.M. (2008). Media policy: The international encyclopedia of communication. *International encyclopedia of communication online*. Retrieved from http://www.communicationencyclopedia.com/subscriber/uid=1714/tocnode?id=g9781405131995_yr2012_chunk_g978140513199518_ss47-1

Postill, J. (2013). *The multilinearity of protest: Understanding new social movements through their events, trends, and routines*. Melbourne: RMIT University. Retrieved from http://johnpostill.com/2013/10/19/the-multilinearity-of-protest/

Scott, J.C. (2014). *Two cheers for anarchism: Six easy pieces on autonomy, dignity, and meaningful work and play*. Princeton, NJ: Princeton University Press.

Street, B. (2003). What's "new" in new literacy studies? *Critical approaches to literacy in theory and practice, 5*(2), 77–91.

Streeter, T. (2013). Policy, politics, and discourse. *Communication, Culture & Critique, 6*(4), 488–501. doi:10.1111/cccr.12028

Wallis, R., & Buckingham, D. (2013). Arming the citizen-consumer: The invention of "media literacy" within UK communications policy. *European Journal of Communication, 28*(5), 527–540. doi:10.1177/0267323113483605

Utopian Games

Greg Lastowka

Games are the dominant medium in which the audience shapes the text. If the future of media is interactive, then that future will likely co-evolve with the video game medium. We are at a pivot point—our goal should be to ensure that our future games transform society for the better, not the worse. Unfortunately, it isn't clear that we can trust the market to provide us with the best games. State, federal, and local governments should become more involved—*constructively* involved—with the creation of video games.

In order to understand the future of games, we need to understand their past. Games are part of our play impulse, a drive that we share will other animals. Play entails a range of practices: ducking out of "ordinary life," ascribing entirely new symbolic meanings to our interactions with objects and others, and adapting behaviors to pursue new forms of success, failure, and progress. Consider chess: two contestants exert their utmost concentration on arranging and rearranging strangely shaped pieces on a gridded board—when a certain configuration is achieved, we declare a winner and a loser. What is the social value of that process?

Roger Caillois (1961) answered that play and games are "pure waste," a view that accords with common (as well as Puritanical) beliefs about play. Games are leisure: playing games does not put food on the table or keep the winter at bay. As Aesop explained, the grasshopper dies and the ants live. Perhaps because of this, academic literature on games has historically featured a diverse hodge-podge of disciplinary approaches. Only when taken as grist for the mills of economics, biology, philosophy, child psychology, anthropological theory, or folklore could the waste of play become a substance worthy of study.

A handful of scholars, however, have set apart and valorized play (as play) in various ways: Johan Huizinga (1950) claimed that play formed the foundation of human civilization. He celebrated our capacity to forget our basest needs (i.e. for food and shelter) and immerse our wills in complex systems of manufactured meanings. He claimed play as the foundation of culture. He saw law, religion, art, and social institutions generally, as very complicated games. Brian Sutton-Smith (1997) lamented the lack of a core discipline of play studies, noting how discourse on games and play devolved into competing and discordant rhetorics. And Bernard Suits (1978) claimed that games were, in essence, utopias; if our base needs were satisfied, instrumental action would become unnecessary and humanity would pursue only intrinsically enjoyable activities. In other words, if we had what we needed, we would play games.

In recent years, "game studies" has gained a small foothold in the academy. This is attributable mostly to money, i.e. the commercial scale of the modern video game industry. Game revenues now rival those of the film and music recording industries, entitling video games to some recognition in departments of communication and media studies. Not coincidentally, it seems the arbiters of culture have taken note as well. *The New Yorker* now includes mentions of *Grand Theft Auto V* and *Candy Crush Saga*, while the Smithsonian and MOMA have hosted earnest exhibits of video games in recent years. Well-known game evangelists, like Jane McGonigal (2011), argue that future games will energize us to change the world and repair the broken state of reality. The holdouts of the *Ancien Régime* may still refuse to seat video games at the table of cultural significance, but who wants to dine with Miss. Havisham anyway?

The technological momentum that brought games to this juncture, however, is largely played out. The mantra of video game evolution has been "realism," but the sort of realism celebrated—more pixels, better physics, throbbing subwoofers—seems to have reached a point of diminishing returns. The market reflects this. *Angry Birds*, *Farmville*, and *Candy Crush Saga* all rejected the forced march to infinite polygon counts. This is not to deny the emergence of the next wave of VR, bandwidth, and processing power—the Oculus Rift headset is certainly neat—but it seems the market is not all about *The Matrix*.

The true heart of the video game is the joy of interaction. Alvin Toffler (1980) noted this, claiming that early consoles like the Atari 2600 were not simply "innocent devices," but were part and parcel of an audience revolution:

> [M]illions of people are learning to play with the television set, to talk back to it, and to interact with it. In the process they are changing from passive receivers to message senders as well. They are manipulating the set rather than merely letting the set manipulate them.

Toffler saw videogames as a medium imbued with a democratizing message. Chris Crawford (1984), an early videogame creator and theorist, agreed: *interactivity* was the key element that separated video games from all prior media. Players are not the audience. Games are not mere spectacle, but an active participation in a reoriented relationship to the world. Motion pictures may benefit (or may not) from super-HD, 3D, surround sound, and Smell-O-Vision—but games are about active performance.

And there's the rub that abrades our political philosophy of games. If games are all about freedom of action, what can the player do? Historically, very little. Our best games have offered a reductive milieu of thought and performance. Two players or teams have contested over an endless parade of variously shaped balls, propelled onward by variously chosen limbs and instruments, seeking various pins, hoops, hands, holes, and nets. So there are variations, but, in essence, all sports are the same: players struggle to control a ball. Video games began with exactly this simplicity: *Pong* was about a ball and two paddles. One of the most recent games *du jour*, *Angry Birds*, is only marginally more complex: birds are loaded, aimed, and flung at a target. *Angry Birds* is bowling—with birds.

Of course, some celebrated games do struggle to free the player, attempting to create a true "open world" environment where anything is possible. *Assassin's Creed IV* and *Grand Theft Auto V* throw the player into rich costume dramas set in the eighteenth-century Caribbean and a seedy parody of twenty-first-century Los Angeles, respectively. Their rendered worlds are certainly more aesthetically compelling than what you'll find in the average bowling alley, and the options for player action are far beyond what you'll find in *Angry Birds*. *Assassin's Creed IV* lets you hunt whales, explore islands, and play Checkers, Fanorona, and Nine Men's Morris. *Grand Theft Auto* offers at least 50 mini-games: from tennis and golf, to investing in the virtual stock market, to listening to the radio, to having your character watch three entirely original movies in three different virtual movie theaters. Ultimately, though, you can't do *anything*—instead you can do hundreds of interesting things, all ultimately anticipated and choreographed by the game developers. Your path of play is on rails—multiple rails, but rails nonetheless.

Skeptics suggest that game developers will always control the path of play. McKenzie Wark (2007) portrays gamers as spiritually blind rats trapped in digital mazes, hooked on the thrill of virtual achievements. Wark's vision of the future anticipates more obsessed gamers flinging more emotionally compelling birds and balls at newer and shinier pigs and nets. Gamers will run and shoot at increasingly lifelike aliens and enemies in pursuit of more breathtaking fireworks and bigger gold stars.

There is certainly something to this: the game industry is currently mapping brain activity and gathering big data on player behavior, convinced that the consumer's mind can be hooked, at some pre-conscious level, by a carefully orchestrated flow of sights, sounds, and achievements. The race is underway to crack the biochemical code of the gaming impulse/addiction. The winner will be the firm seated squarely at the bottleneck in the endorphin rush supply chain. So much for Toffler's vision: future players will not be manipulating the set, they will let the set manipulate them.

To top off this dystopia, just mix in the next iterations of *Call of Duty*, *Battlefield*, *Halo*, and *Team Fortress*. Gamers will perform increasingly effective and efficient acts of violence in increasingly realistic and addictive settings. Weapons will be rendered with meticulous care, while the post-game realities of working with the VA hospitals, finding a job, and struggling with PTSD will be elided. The true dystopian vision of the future is players racing faster and faster on the developer's rails, locked in their path by carefully tuned algorithms that serve the military-industrial-entertainment complex or some equivalent hegemon. The Brave New World of gaming will be the perfectly gilded cage, an elaborate technocratic Skinner Box (Yee, 2014). Is this the endpoint of interactive media?

Not necessarily. To re-craft a utopian vision of games, we can stress another meaning of play: freedom. This is the "play" of slackness—freedom to stray from fixed coordinates. This sort of play can even worm its way into first person shooters. Anne-Marie Schleiner painted pink teddy bears and hearts on the walls of the *Counterstrike* game, using the tools provided to protest the game's militaristic fantasy (Huntemann & Payne, 2009). Joseph DeLappe logged into the *America's Army* game and recited a list of soldiers killed in Iraq on the in-game chat channel. Just because a game gives you a gun doesn't mean you have to shoot it. Interactivity is freedom, which entails freedom to run your train off the rails.

In theory, players are also free to choose those games with rails running in the right direction. If the federally funded game *America's Army* was effective at recruiting and training soldiers, there's no reason that state-sponsored games can't serve other instrumental purposes, such as education, science, and civic virtue. *Oregon Trail*, for instance, is a fondly recalled early video game designed to illustrate the challenges faced by American pioneers—the *Assassin's Creed* series, at its best, can offer similar knowledge of past events. *Foldit* is a game developed by the University of Washington that allows online players to solve complex problems involving the folding of proteins. Some player solutions have led to new scientific discoveries. *Macon Money* provided two half-pieces of a newly minted community currency to two strangers in Macon, Georgia. By finding each other, players built community solidarity and increased the patronage of local businesses.

But the most tantalizing form of freedom is the freedom to lay one's own rails. Some of the most popular toys in the National Toy Hall of Fame are the box (inducted 2005), the stick (2008), and the blanket (2011). Play and games, at their best, are about reimagining the world and making one's own rules. Games like Sony's *LittleBIGPlanet*, Mojang's *Minecraft*, and Valve's *Garry's Mod* let players build their own games. *Minecraft* is the best example. It has been wildly successful with a wide demographic range despite the fact that it was created by an unknown Swedish programmer, had no advertising budget, enjoyed no venture capital backing, and wasn't even finished when it took the internet by storm. For all the things it lacked, it also lacked rails. And that was its genius.

Minecraft and games like it are sometimes called "sandboxes," alluding to a well-known offline analogic set of childhood play practices. The appeal of *Minecraft* is the same as the appeal of the box, the stick, the ball, and the blanket. *Minecraft* players build, explore, and negotiate with other players about how to best harvest, share, and spend resources. What makes *Minecraft* so attractive to its players is the lack of rails—the play is digital, but it is primarily the play of freedom.

The goal for those concerned about the future of games is to ensure that they support this sort of freedom. It is hardly clear that the market will deliver that freedom. The motion picture industry, which is increasingly intertwined with the game industry, knows narrative and spectacle, not play. Markets and intellectual property laws celebrate and incentivize consumer consumption, not consumer empowerment. Consider the market evolution of Lego®, and despair: the freedom to play with a set of bricks has steadily lost ground to brands, copyrights, patents, and cross-licensing arrangements. Lego® once offered an open world game, but the demands of the market pushed it toward the rails of commercial exploitation.

Video games are at a pivot point. If we want to create technologies of freedom, we need to appreciate not just the value of games, but also the politics embedded in games. It would be wonderful if our current market-driven, laissez-faire approach to media development would provide us with utopian games. But it won't. The best games of the future will be true public goods, and markets have not excelled at providing those. Given the extreme scale of existing civic subsidies for sports stadia, collegiate athletics, high-school football, and the Olympics, it is clear that governments are willing to subsidize games. If we care about the future of media, we should encourage the government to come up with a vision of good games. And then, as a polity, we should spend some serious time and money building better video games.

References

Caillois, R. (1961). *Man, play, and games.* New York, NY: Free Press of Glencoe.
Crawford, C. (1984). *The art of computer game design: Reflections of a master game designer.* Berkeley, CA: Osborne/McGraw-Hill.
Huizinga, J. (1950). *Homo ludens: A study of the play element in culture.* Boston, MA: Beacon Press.
Huntemann, N.B., & Payne, M.T. (2009). *Joystick soldiers: The politics of play in military video games.* New York, NY: Routledge.
McGonigal, J. (2011). *Reality is broken: Why games make us better and how they can change the world.* New York, NY: Penguin Press HC.
Suits, B.H. (1978). *The grasshopper: Games, life, and utopia.* Toronto: University of Toronto Press.
Sutton-Smith, B. (1997). *The ambiguity of play.* Cambridge, MA: Harvard University Press.
Toffler, A. (1980). *The third wave.* New York, NY: Morrow.
Wark, M. (2007). *Gamer theory.* Cambridge, MA: Harvard University Press.
Yee, N. (2014). *The proteus paradox: How online games and virtual worlds change us, and how they don't.* New Haven, CT: Yale University Press.

Fair Use Goes Global

Peter Decherney

For 150 years, fair use was a solely American doctrine. But in the 1990s and 2000s, the Philippines, Israel, and South Korea all adopted American-style fair use. Since then, debates have erupted over whether or not to introduce fair use into the copyright laws of a half dozen additional countries, including the Netherlands, Canada, the United Kingdom, Japan, and Australia. Why is fair use going global? What do innovators, scholars, and legislators see in the fair use doctrine? And what is tipping the scale in favor of or against fair use? We don't yet know whether the global fair use movement will fizzle out or take over world intellectual property regimes. But looking at the debates over the global spread of fair use, even at this early stage, tells us a lot about digital media's challenge to the regulation of both technological innovation and online expression.

For 150 years, fair use was a solely American doctrine. But in the 1990s and 2000s, the Philippines, Israel, and South Korea all adopted American-style fair use.[1] Since then, debates have erupted over whether or not to introduce fair use into the copyright laws of a half dozen additional countries, including the Netherlands, Canada, the United Kingdom, Japan, and Australia. Why is fair use going global? What do innovators, scholars, and legislators see in the fair use doctrine? And what is tipping the scale in favor of or against fair use? We don't yet know whether the global fair use movement will fizzle out or take over world intellectual property regimes. But looking at the debates over the global spread of fair use, even at this early stage, tells us a lot about digital media's challenge to the regulation of both technological innovation and online expression.

Fair Use Today

Fair use, simply, is the exception that allows for the reuse of copyrighted material without permission—at least in certain situations. I frequently hear the perpetuation

92

of myths like "all commercial uses are not fair uses" or "all educational uses are fair uses."[2] Neither proposition is true, and just about any sentence that begins with the word "all" is doomed to represent a fallacy about fair use. Fair use is widely misunderstood in part because it refuses to stand still. Especially since the 1990s, fair use has changed dramatically. Case law regarding the reuse of copyrighted work has shifted from emphasizing the market impact to the purpose of the reuse. Second Circuit Court of Appeals Judge Pierre Leval first labeled this interpretation of the fair use doctrine "transformative use," (Leval, 1990) and the phrase has caught on. The Supreme Court relied on the transformative use test in its 1994 *Campbell v Accuff Rose* decision (510 U.S. 569), and ever since fair use determinations have increasingly hinged on the extent to which works repurpose and recontextualize the copyrighted material that they quote.

Examples of transformative use include playing an excerpt of a popular song during a public lecture about music, quoting snippets of news articles in search engine results, and reediting a television episode to highlight the activity of a minor character. In all of these examples, the quoted work is being used for a new purpose: a popular song is used for education instead of entertainment, excerpts of news stories are displayed to help users find the best information, and a reedited television show comments on popular culture. These uses are likely to be fair uses even if there is a commercial aspect to their use. Indeed, many landmark fair use cases involve commercial uses, since it is large companies that have the motivation and means to litigate.[3] From the development of technological giants like Google to the fan-made mashup videos that draw millions of viewers to video sharing sites, fair use has been a major driver of internet technology, culture, and commerce. And policy stakeholders in many countries have seen an innovation gap created by their lack of a fair use provision.

Exporting Silicon Valley

Is the spread of fair use just another American export in a globalized economy, like Starbucks or Lady Gaga? To hear United Kingdom Prime Minister David Cameron talk about fair use, you might think so. In the wake of the 2008 financial crisis, Cameron's government looked for ways to stimulate the British economy, and it settled on a plan to emulate the success of Northern California's Silicon Valley. Silicon Valley had already spawned competitors in Bangalore, India; Daejeon, South Korea; and Zhongguancun, China, among other cities that claimed the "Silicon Valley of" mantle for their region. Cameron wanted the Shoreditch section of east London to be next in line, the first British "Silicon Roundabout." Clearly a devotee of social theorist Richard Florida's work on the creative class and urban renewal (Florida, 2002), Cameron pointed out that Shoreditch already had the bohemian culture that seems to be a prerequisite for a tech boom. Cameron planned to introduce the necessary policy overhauls as well, including immigration reform and, yes, fair use (Cameron, 2010). Cameron expressed concern that Google could not have been started in the U.K., because its indexing of the web relies on fair use. "Over there," Cameron said referring to the United States,

> they have what are called "fair-use" provisions, which some people believe gives companies more breathing space to create new products and services. So I can announce today that we are reviewing our [intellectual property] laws, to see if we can make them fit for the internet age. I want to encourage the sort of creative innovation that exists in America. (Cameron, 2010)

Fair use has indeed allowed for the creation of new technologies from the VCR to the iPod to the still controversial Slingbox set top devices that bring digital video to phones and tablets. U.S. copyright law has aided in the development of these technologies, because it provides what Google copyright lawyer Fred von Lohmann calls "fair use startup capital." (von Lohmann, 2008). Fair use acknowledges that innovation requires the ability to build on existing technologies and find creative ways of distributing and reusing media. Debates about how to measure the contributions of fair use and the copyright industries to the U.S. GDP will continue to rage (Word Intellectual Property Organization, 2012; Rogers & Szamosszegi, 2010), but it is clear that fair use has created entire new industries and greatly expands the reach of existing media companies. The paradigm here is, of course, the VCR which appeared first as a threat to and then the savior of Hollywood (Decherney, 2012). It is not surprising that the first two countries outside the U.S. to adopt fair use are also two of the most active innovators in the field of digital technology: Israel and South Korea. Israel has been dubbed the "startup nation," because it hosts more tech startup companies per capita than any other country. From text messaging protocols to semiconductor chip design, it is difficult to use a cell phone or computer without relying on a technology developed in Israel. Fair use is also in line with many of the organizational structures of Israeli high tech companies, as Dan Senor and Saul Singer have described them. Israel's tech companies, in particular, tend to be non-hierarchical, focusing on bottom up innovation and collaborative problem solving (Senor & Singer, 2009) Fair use embodies a related collaborative ethos. It is premised on the idea that a bit of permissionless reuse facilitates the generation of new ideas and expands markets for all, where a closed permission-based society thwarts new entrants with little power or capital.

South Korea has also been a leading developer of digital technologies and internet policy innovations. The Korean government jumpstarted its tech boom by building out a large and superfast broadband network in order to spur the development of internet technologies and speed up their adoption among consumers. Both goals seem to have been met successfully. One recent study, for example, ranked Korea first in "digital natives" with 99.6% of Korean young people active internet users for five or more years (Pfanner, 2013). As the Korean government provided a shared broadband infrastructure—a commons—on which its citizens could deploy and access new technologies, it has adopted fair use with the expectation that a certain amount of shared infrastructure is part of a successful climate for innovation.

David Cameron's "Silicon Roundabout" speech did lead to two large-scale studies of the United Kingdom's intellectual property laws, the Gowers Review of Intellectual Property (2006) and the Hargreaves report (2011). The recommendations from those studies call for some far-reaching reforms, though they ultimately reject the adoption of fair use, because they claim it is incompatible with existing U.K. law. Moreover, the Hargreaves report downplays the importance of fair use, noting that "Silicon Valley owes more to attitudes to business risk and investor culture, not to mention other complex issues of economic geography, than it does to IP law" (Hargreaves, 2011, p. 45). Perhaps the report is correct, but just because the U.K. cannot reproduce every aspect of Silicon Valley's success is not a reason to reject one ingredient of the recipe. It is interesting to note that although Shoreditch has developed into a kind of "Silicon Roundabout," Google, Facebook, and other U.S. companies—many deeply reliant of fair use—tend to dominate it.

Freedom to Mashup

In addition to facilitating high tech development, fair use has a long history of promoting free speech and debate in the U.S, a function that has become especially apparent since the advent of YouTube, iTunes (think podcasts and iTunes U), and other media sharing outlets. During the 2008 presidential election, for example, both the Obama–Biden and McCain–Palin campaigns employed their YouTube channels to reach voters and quickly respond to their opponents, often invoking fair use when excerpting news reports and speeches. In a letter to YouTube, the General Counsel of the McCain–Palin campaign defended the campaign's videos as "paradigmatic examples of fair use," while expressing frustration that copyright holders kept asking to have them removed (Potter, 2008). Scholars and legislators in the Netherlands and the European Union more generally have begun to worry that without fair use an expression gap is developing in addition to an innovation gap. Without fair use, Europeans are not able to participate fully in the growing public sphere of debate on YouTube, Vimeo, and other sharing networks. Intellectual property expert Bernt Hugenoholtz has been one of the leading voices in favor of importing fair use to the EU. Hugenoholtz has worried about the inability of EU citizens to take part in the important discussions occurring online. Many of the videos we find [on YouTube], he writes,

> are creative remixes of material protected under copyright. They're mostly for laughs or political commentary … If we applied the law today strictly, we would not be allowed to do these things [in Europe] … Freedom is a good thing … But in Europe, where we do not have open norms like the fair use doctrine in the United States, we can't do these things without infringing the law. (Hugenholtz, quoted in Chesal, 2012)

Hugenholtz is well aware of the complications of harmonizing fair use and European intellectual property directives. Nevertheless, he argues that, "[t]he current lack of flexibility in [EU] copyright law undermines the very fundamental freedoms, societal interests and economic goals that copyright law traditionally aims to protect and advance" (Hugenholtz & Senftleben, 2011). Copyright, in other words, should promote rather than deter creative production, and copyright law has historically been updated to accommodate new modes of creativity (Decherney, 2012).

Just as fair use creates a form of startup capital for technology businesses, it underpins modes of expression that are becoming important outlets for political speech online. And governments that do not want their citizens to be left out of the conversation will have to seriously consider developing a fair use standard. Another option is to create specific statutory exceptions for important modes of expression like parody or online platforms like YouTube. But creating narrow exemptions has proven to be politically controversial, and the legislative process is destined to lag behind innovation in cultural expression.

What's Not to Like?

If it promotes the development of new technologies and creative expression, what is not to like about fair use? A common concern is that fair use in the United States has had over a century and a half to evolve. Fair use, like other case law, is built on example, and moving from no fair use one day to active fair use the next might cause chaos and confusion. This has been a concern of the Motion Picture Association of America—never fair use's biggest cheerleader—and the organization has warned the Australian government about this issue in an official comment on their deliberations about adopting fair use (Motion Picture Association of America, 2013).

Luckily, we already have two examples of countries, Israel and South Korea, that have adopted fair use standards. One phenomenon that we can identify is the replaying of American fair use cases, though often with culturally specific facts and conclusions. In Israel, for example, all uses of copyrighted material that claim fair use must also include attribution of the original work. Attribution is not a requirement for fair use in the United States This adaptation of fair use draws on the rights of attribution present in continental moral rights as well as the ancient Jewish exegetical insistence on citing the authorities that scholars respond to and comment on.

One Korean fair use case in particular seemed to replay a highly publicized U.S. case. In the Korean case, a music label sent a takedown notice to a man who posted a video of his son imitating a popular dance from a K-pop music video. (K-pop is an abbreviation for the South Korean popular music movement brought to international attention by Psy's song "Gangham Style.") This fair use case involved a boy imitating a widely parodied "chair dance" from the video for musician Son Dam-bi's song "Crazy." The boy's father brought the case to court, filing for a declaratory judgment— a ruling on copyright holder's claims that his son's dance required permission. It is a case that reminded some of a U.S. case involving a YouTube video of a young boy dancing to the Prince song "Let's Go Crazy" (*Lenz* v *Universal*)—even the song names—"Crazy" and "Let's Go Crazy"—were uncannily similar. The Prince case is still being litigated, but so far courts have found it to be a clear fair use. In the Korean case, the court strongly agreed. "If this kind of User Generated Content is barred from uploading online," the judge wrote, "it results in a unnecessarily excessive restraint on the free expression." The Korean court also ordered the copyright holder to pay the father for "mental damages suffered from the takedown" (Masnick, 2010). Again, we see fair use emerging as an important engine for new genres of expression in online environments. And we see that countries new to fair use have been able to forge their own models of the doctrine, promoting cultural specific values.

Googlization, Good or Evil

The global spread of fair use may tell another story as well, one of money and power. Media scholar Siva Vaidhyanathan warns us about the potential "Googlization of Everything" (Vaidhyanathan, 2011), and cynics might see the global spread of fair use as simply another front in Google's takeover of the digital world. Google has been a strong proponent of fair use, which underlies much of its business model and functionality from its search engine to YouTube. And Google has continually been thwarted by copyright law outside the United States (see, for example, Carr, 2012). In response, Google has greatly expanded its lobbying offices both inside and outside the United States and Google's lobbyists and legal teams have actively advocated for fair use internationally. Google is certainly one force behind the globalization of fair use, and their attention is obviously self-interested. But it may be an instance in which Google's self-interest is in line with a policy initiative that supports the next wave of global technological, political, commercial, and artistic innovation. In any case, we have a rare opportunity to follow the diffusion of the global fair use experiment and measure the value of fair use for countries that adopt it, for countries that reject it, and for the control group, the United States.

Notes

[1] While the Philippines does have a fair use standard, it seems to be largely dormant.
[2] See, for example, discussions of fair use on Quora.com.
[3] See, for example, *Suntrust* v *Houghton Mifflin*, 268 F.3d 1257 (11th Cir. 2001), and *Bill Graham Archives* v *Dorling Kindersley*, 448 F.3d 605, (2d Cir. 2006).

References

Cameron, D. (2010, November 4). David Cameron sets out Britain's hi-tech future. *Wired.co.uk*.

Campbell v Accuff Rose (1994) 510 U.S. 569. http://www.wired.co.uk/news/archive/2010-11/04/david-cameron-silicon-roundabout

Carr, D. (2012, November 4). Publishers abroad take on Google. *New York Times*. http://www.nytimes.com/2012/11/05/business/media/google-news-faces-challenges-from-publishers-abroad.html?pagewanted=all

Chesal, R. (2012, February 13). Loosen up copyright law, says Dutch government. Radio Netherlands Worldwide. http://www.rnw.nl/english/article/loosen-copyright-law-says-dutch-government

Decherney, P. (2012). *Hollywood's copyright wars: From Edison to the internet*. New York, NY: Columbia University Press.

Florida, R. (2002). *The rise of the creative class: And how It's transforming work, leisure, community and everyday life*. New York, NY: Basic Books.

Gowers, A. (2006). *Gowers review of intellectual property*. London: HM Treasury.

Hargreaves, I. (2011, May). *Digital opportunity: A review of intellectual property and growth*. London: UK Intellectual Property Office.

Hugenholtz, P. B., & Senftleben, M. (2011). Fair use in Europe: In Search of flexibilities. Amsterdam: Vrije University Working Paper.

Lenz v Universal (2008). 572 F. Supp. 2d 1150.

Leval, P. N. (1990, March). Toward a fair use standard. *Harvard Law Review, 103*, 1105–1136. doi:10.2307/1341457

Masnick, M. (2010, October 13). Korea gets its own dancing baby copyright fight: Says free expression trumps copyright concern. *TechDirt*. http://www.techdirt.com/articles/20101005/12244 211297/korea-gets-its-own-dancing-baby-copyright-fight-says-free-expression-trumps-copyright-concern.shtml

Motion Picture Association of America Inc. (2013, July 30). Submission to the Australian Law Reform Commission. http://www.alrc.gov.au/sites/default/files/subs/573._org_motion_picture_association_of_america_inc.jul31.pdf

Pfanner, E. (2013, October 7). Young people are not as digitally native as you Think. *The New York Times, Bits Blog*. http://bits.blogs.nytimes.com/2013/10/07/young-people-are-not-as-digitally-native-as-you-think/

Potter, T. (2008, October 13). Letter to Chad Hurley, YouTube. http://www.eff.org/files/McCain% 20YouTube%20copyright%20letter%2010.13.08.pdf

Rogers, T., & Szamosszegi, A. (2010). Fair use in the U.S. economy: Economic contribution of industries relying on fair use. Washington, DC: Computer & Communications Industry Association.

Senor, D., & Singer, S. (2009). *Start-up nation: The story of Israel's economic miracle*. New York, NY: Twelve.

Vaidhyanathan, S. (2011). *The Googlization of everything (and why we should worry)*. Berkeley: University of California.

von Lohmann, F. (2008). Fair use and innovation policy. *Berkeley Technology Law Journal, 23*, 829–865.

World Intellectual Property Organization. (2012). Copyright + Creativity = Jobs and Economic Growth. http://www.ip-watch.org/weblog/wp-content/uploads/2012/02/WIPO-Copyright-Economic-Contribution-Analysis-2012-FINAL-230-2.pdf

The Great Evasion: Confronting Market Failure in American Media Policy

Victor Pickard

The history of American media is in many ways a history of market failure. Yet these recurring patterns almost always go unrecognized in mainstream policy discourse. Because media are special kinds of goods and services, the market's failure to provide them is particularly deleterious for democratic governance. The "public good" qualities and other characteristics intrinsic to media result in a kind of systemic market failure that cannot be entirely eliminated. However, this market failure can be reduced or compensated for via public policy that recognizes the tremendous positive externalities associated with a healthy media system.

A historical view of American media lays bare discernible patterns: over-commercialization, concentrated ownership, lack of diversity, poor access, and weak public service traditions. With alarming regularity, many of these deficiencies recur with each new commercial medium, from the telegraph to the internet. These trends are often bound up in a phenomenon known as "market failure," which generally refers to the market's inability to efficiently allocate important goods and services (Taylor, 2007, p. 15). The history of American media is in many ways a history of market failure (Pickard, in press), yet these recurring patterns almost always go unrecognized in mainstream policy discourse. Because media are special kinds of goods and services, the market's failure to provide them is particularly deleterious for democratic governance. As I elaborate below, the "public good" qualities and other characteristics intrinsic to media result in a kind of systemic market failure that cannot be entirely eliminated. However, this market failure can be reduced or compensated for via public policy that recognizes the tremendous positive externalities associated with a healthy media system.

According to textbook scenarios, cases of market failure should necessitate public policy intervention. This necessity, however, is usually obscured by what I refer to as "corporate libertarianism"—an ideological project that equates corporations' freedoms generally, and media firms' privileges specifically, with individual liberties like First Amendment protections. Such an arrangement renders state interventions on behalf of public interest protections as *a priori* illegitimate. Therefore, we cannot dare talk about market failure because to do so may suggest that the government should intervene. The following essay posits that market failure should become a central concern within policy discourse. Such a refocusing, I argue, would help justify targeted government interventions, thereby realigning media policy with democratic values like equal access to diverse information and media production.

Media as Public Goods

The argument that the information produced by news media should be treated as a public good has gained greater visibility in recent years, especially as the journalism crisis has worsened (Baker, 2002, p. 8; Hamilton, 2006, pp. 8–9; Pickard, Stearns, & Aaron, 2009, pp. 1–9; McChesney & Nichols, 2010, pp. 101–103; Pickard, 2011, p. 89). Because public goods are non-rivalrous (one person's consumption does not detract from another's) and non-excludable (difficult to monetize and to exclude from free riders), they differ from other commodities, like cars or clothes, within a capitalistic economy (Samuelson, 1954). As one economist put it, "it is virtually impossible to allocate a pure public good through market mechanisms" (Trogen, 2005, p. 169). Many public goods—like artificial light, clean air, knowledge—also produce positive externalities (benefits that accrue to parties outside of the direct economic transaction) that are essential for a healthy society. In this sense, the information produced by journalistic practices is a public good that carries tremendous positive externalities because it confers social benefits beyond its revenue stream. As an essential public service, news media ideally serve as an adversarial watchdog over the powerful, a forum for diverse voices and viewpoints, and a rich information source for important social issues upon which citizens will vote.

Like many public goods exhibiting positive externalities, journalism has never been fully supported by direct market transactions; it always has been subsidized to some degree. Since the late 19th century, journalism has been primarily supported by advertising revenues. But this model is increasingly unsustainable as audiences and advertisers migrate to the internet, where ads sell for a mere fraction of their paper-based counterparts. Although increasing, digital ad revenues are not offsetting enormous losses from traditional advertising. A 2012 Pew study found that declines in print ad revenue, which had fallen more than 50 percent since 2003, far exceeded any gain in online digital revenue, with the ratio of losses to gains greater than 10 to 1 (Edmonds, Guskin, Rosenstiel, & Mitchell, 2012). Despite some stabilization by 2013, Pew found that the growth in digital advertising still "does not come close to covering print ad losses" (Edmonds, Guskin, Mitchell, & Jurkowitz, 2013). Based on these and other data, ad-revenue-dependent models for supporting viable journalism appear to be increasingly unviable, with no other commercial models—like online subscriptions (Pickard & Williams, 2013)—filling the vacuum. The ongoing disinvestment in news production is demonstrated by drastic actions like cutting staff and reducing home deliveries of leading metro dailies such as the *Cleveland Plain Dealer* and the *New Orleans Times-Picayune*—the latter in a city where approximately a third of its residents lack internet connectivity.

Lack of quality internet access brings us to another breakdown in public good provision. Nearly a third of all U.S. households still lack broadband internet, at least partly owing to prohibitive cost (Pew Research Center, 2013). Even for those with access, services are subpar and costly in a global comparison. American broadband is the 7th most expensive, and 19th in terms of speed among leading democracies. In terms of internet penetration, the U.S. ranks 15th internationally, having dropped sharply over the past decade (Organization for Economic Cooperation and Development, 2012). In terms of cost, the U.S. ranked 30th out of 33 countries, with an average price of $90/month for higher speeds of 45 Mbps and over (Geoghegan, 2013). The average American broadband customer currently pays over $40/month for 27 Mbps, while an average South Korean pays a fraction of that price for 70 Mbps (Organization for Economic Cooperation and Development, 2011). A more recent report exposes the degree to which American cities lag behind their counterparts around the world in broadband speeds and prices. For example, the same broadband speed that fetches $21.75 in Riga, Latvia, costs $112.50 in Washington, D.C. (Hussain, Kehl, Lucey, & Russo, 2013).

These inequities are neither happenstance nor inevitable; they result from explicit policies that accommodate oligopolistic markets and corporate interests in general (McChesney, 2013; Crawford, 2013). Such are the predictable outcomes of a political process captured by commercial power. And this regulatory capture leads to a kind of discursive capture reflected in a corporate libertarian paradigm that masks market failures and discredits government intervention.

Evading Market Failure

The inadequacy of commercial support for democracy-sustaining infrastructures suggests what should be obvious by now: the systematic underproduction of vital communications like journalistic media and accessible, affordable, and reliable broadband internet services qualifies as a clear case of market failure. Although this analytical framework derives from neoclassical economic theory—where it is often treated as a rare event—market failure has also been a concern among critical political economists who focus on media's normative foundations and who observe a number of market failures affecting media specifically. For example, commercial media markets tend toward concentration and produce both negative and positive externalities that must be managed via government regulation (Freedman, 2008, pp. 8–9). Positive externalities especially come into play with the consumption of "merit goods," which are goods that society requires, but that individuals typically undervalue (are unable or unwilling to pay for), and thus the market under-produces (Musgrave, 1959, pp. 13–15; Leys, 2001, pp. 97–98; Ali, 2013). Such market failures typically occur when private enterprise withholds investments in critical social services because it cannot extract the returns that would justify expenditures, or when consumers fail to pay for such services' full societal benefit.

The leading consumer advocate and researcher Mark Cooper (2011) demonstrates that various kinds of "pervasive market failure" specifically affect the media industry. In addition to the lack of support for public goods, positive externalities constitute a separate market failure whereby consumers do not support services that are socially beneficial. Another kind of market failure that frequently occurs in the American media system is associated with structural flaws like oligopolistic concentration and profit maximization. Uncompetitive markets can lead to perverse incentives and the abuse of market power, which results in a media system's overall degradation. In addition to noting the problems with monopolies, public goods, and externalities, Cooper makes the important point that commercial media markets typically fail to ensure interconnection between networks and to provide communication services to all of society, which can lead to red-lining (privileging profitable markets and communities over others). Other kinds of market failure involving media include information asymmetries, and problems with economies of scale and scope like high first-copy costs (Baker, 2002, p. 9).

While market failure in the American media system is increasingly visible, the vocabulary for describing such structural problems remains impoverished. Similar situations requiring state intervention to ensure essential services and infrastructures not sufficiently provided by the market include public education, a standing military, and a national highway system. That the government provides for these services is largely naturalized and rarely requires justification. Yet it generally remains counterintuitive that the same rationale can be used to justify enacting public policy to address failures in media markets. Although its relationship to market failure is rarely stated, the foundation of a public broadcasting system is an example of this logic put into practice. Similarly, having a category for "public interest" policies implicitly acknowledges endemic market failure in commercial media. Nonetheless, an explicit discussion of these political economic relationships has remained virtually nonexistent among policymakers. Whether appraising the lack of support for local journalism or deficiencies in providing universal access to affordable and reliable internet service, a focus on market failure deserves more prominence in American media policy discourse.

Structural Interventions and Alternative Infrastructures

Once market failure is acknowledged at the discursive level, it can be treated as a social problem that warrants public policy intervention. However, whereas a neoclassical economist might argue for simply fostering more competition to create the desired outcomes, what I refer to as "systemic media market failure" calls for additional policy interventions to ensure that a media system's positive externalities are supported and enhanced. Potential remedies include anti-monopoly structural interventions like antitrust measures to increase competition as well as significant investments in alternative, non-profit, and noncommercial communication infra-structures to promote structural diversity. This muscular policy approach is called for because oligopolistic media firms otherwise have little incentive to make the necessary investments to address structural problems like insufficient capacity.

A first step toward a partial remedy is to subsidize the build-out of alternative communication networks to compete with incumbent internet service providers. Susan Crawford (2013) makes a compelling argument that digital media industries wield such influence over the political process that structural intervention like trust-busting is virtually impossible for the immediate future. However, she sees hope in a smattering of community owned internet networks that provide cheap and reliable broadband services to their residents, thereby challenging the dominance of providers such as Verizon and Comcast—at least in the 31 states that have not yet passed laws making it extremely difficult or impossible for municipalities to offer community broadband. Locally owned and controlled wireless or municipal fiber internet networks could be operated through community media centers. These centers could be housed in post offices or public libraries and supported by local and national tax revenues. This community media infrastructure could also help produce journalistic media by combining resources with public radio stations, public access television, low power FM radio, and other local institutions.

While addressing market failure within the digital realm would greatly benefit news media, policy reforms aimed specifically at lessening market pressures on journalistic institutions could help liberate them to become more focused on adversarial reporting and more accountable to diverse communities. A three-pronged approach to reinventing journalism would involve subsidies for an expanded public media system, tax incentives for struggling media institutions to transition into low- and non-profit status, and government-sponsored research and development efforts for new digital models that may include public/private hybrids. Together, these initiatives would remove or reduce market pressures and help restore journalism's public service mission (Pickard, in press).

Before any of these reforms can occur, American policy discourse must first be reframed to acknowledge systemic media market failure. The ongoing evasion of this structural critique will likely perpetuate worsening communication inequalities in the U.S. Transitioning to a new digital media system requires a paradigm shift away from corporate libertarianism toward a framework that recognizes media's public good qualities and positive externalities, and embraces government's affirmative role in providing for society's communication needs. A long-standing "American exception-alism" in media policy discourse assumes almost no legitimate role—aside from servicing business interests—for government intervention in media markets. Until American media's deficiencies are confronted as market failure, policymakers and reformers will be forced to contend with the pathology's symptoms instead of its root problems.

References

Ali, C. (2013). Where is here? An analysis of localism in media policy in three western democracies (Unpublished Ph.D. dissertation, University of Pennsylvania, U.S.).

Baker, C.E. (2002). *Media, markets and democracy*. New York, NY: Cambridge University Press.

Cooper, M. (2011). The future of journalism: Addressing pervasive market failure with public policy. In R. McChesney & V. Pickard (Eds.), *Will the last reporter please turn out the lights* (pp. 320–339). New York, NY: New Press.

Crawford, S. (2013). *Captive audience: The telecom industry and monopoly power in the new gilded age*. New Haven, CT: Yale University Press.

Edmonds, R., Guskin, E., Rosenstiel, T., & Mitchell, A. (2012). Newspapers: By the numbers. *The Pew Research Center's project for excellence in journalism: The state of the news media 2012*. Retrieved from http://stateofthemedia.org

Edmonds, R., Guskin, E., Mitchell, A., & Jurkowitz, M. (2013). *The Pew Research Center's project for excellence in journalism: The state of the news media 2013*. Retrieved from http://stateofthemedia.org/2013/newspapers-stabilizing-but-still-threatened/

Freedman, D. (2008). *The politics of media policy*. Cambridge: Polity Press.

Geoghegan, T. (2013, October 27). Why is broadband more expensive in the US? *BBC News Magazine*. Retrieved from http://www.bbc.co.uk/news/magazine-24528383

Hamilton, J. (2006). *All the news that's fit to sell*. Princeton, NJ: Princeton University Press.

Hussain, H., Kehl, D., Lucey, P., & Russo, N. (2013). The cost of connectivity 2013 data release: A comparison of high-speed internet prices in 24 cities around the world. *New America Foundation*. Retrieved from http://oti.newamerica.net/publications/policy/the_cost_of_connectivity_2013

Leys, C. (2001). *Market-driven politics*. London: Verso.

McChesney, R. (2013). *Digital disconnect: How capitalism is turning the internet against democracy*. New York, NY: New Press.

McChesney, R., & Nichols, J. (2010). *The death and life of American journalism: The media revolution that will begin the world again*. New York, NY: Nation Books.

Musgrave, R. (1959). *The theory of public finance: A study in public economy*. New York, NY: McGraw-Hill.

Organization for Economic Cooperation and Development. (2011). *Average advertised download speeds, by country*. Retrieved from http://www.oecd.org/sti/broadband/BB-Portal_5a_13July_Final.xls

Organization for Economic Cooperation and Development. (2012). *Fixed and wireless broadband subscriptions per 100 inhabitants*. Retrieved from http://www.oecd.org/sti/broadband/1d-OECD-WiredWirelessBB-2012-12_v2.xls

Pew Research Center. (2013). *Home broadband 2013*. Retrieved from http://pewinternet.org/Reports/2013/Broadband.aspx

Pickard, V. (2011). Can government support the press? Historicizing and internationalizing a policy approach to the journalism crisis. *The Communication Review*, *14*(2), 73–95.

Pickard, V. (2013). Social democracy or corporate libertarianism? Conflicting media policy narratives in the wake of market failure. *Communication Theory*, *23*, 336–355.

Pickard, V. (in press). *America's battle for media democracy: The triumph of corporate libertarianism and the future of media reform*. New York, NY: Cambridge University Press.

Pickard, V., & Williams, A. (2013). Salvation or folly? The promises and perils of digital paywalls. *Digital Journalism*, *2*, 195–213.

Pickard, V., Stearns, J., & Aaron, C. (2009). *Saving the news: Toward a national journalism strategy*. Washington, DC: Free Press.

Samuelson, P. (1954). The pure theory of public expenditure. *Review of Economics and Statistics, 36*, 387–389.

Taylor, J. (2007). *Economics* (5th ed.). New York, NY: Houghton Mifflin.

Trogen, P. (2005). Public goods. In D. Robbins (Ed.), *Handbook of public sector economics* (pp. 169–207). New York, NY: Taylor & Francis.

The Death and Life of a Great American Agency

Kevin Werbach

Over the next few years, the Federal Communications Commission (FCC) will go down one of two paths. Its importance may fade to insignificance. Or the FCC may recast its mission and affirm the areas in which it retains unique expertise to address vital questions for the communications future. There are some problems that competition does not solve and general-purpose statutory frameworks do not address. These fall into three broad categories, each of which represents an enduring rationale for an expert regulatory agency: sectoral expertise, interconnection, and vestigial scarcities. The FCC should be as relevant as ever in a converged digital world of endless abundance. It just needs to redefine its objectives in order to maintain its relevance.

Through the past eight decades of electronic media in the U.S., one constant has been the Federal Communications Commission (FCC). Yet the FCC's continued survival is not assured. As communications and media platforms converge into a digital broadband amalgam, the case for a sector-specific regulator suddenly appears uncertain. There have been many political attacks on the FCC over the years. However, the agency has never faced such a basic challenge to its role.

In the coming years, the FCC will go down one of two paths. Its importance may fade to insignificance. Or the FCC may recast its mission, and affirm its unique expertise to address vital questions for the communications and media future.

Standing behind abstract terms such as "public interest," the essential justification for the FCC has always been scarcity. The FCC regulates access to wireless spectrum because the airwaves are seen as inherently scarce (Hazlett, 1990). Based on that authority, it regulates both the market structure and the content available through broadcast media. It was tasked to oversee telecommunications networks because they were viewed as natural monopolies over essential services, with massive fixed costs and powerful network effects deterring real competition (Nuechterlein & Weiser, 2013). These scarcity rationales remain the analytical foundations for the agency's legal authority and its policy initiatives.

Today, we live in an era not of scarcity but of abundance. Instead of three broadcast networks and a handful of local radio stations, Americans have access to hundreds of channels on cable or satellite, and oceans of additional programming online. Wireless technology allows spectrum sharing, obviating the need for government to assign the airwaves rigidly. Instead of Ma Bell as the monopoly telephone provider for most of the U.S., there are cable operators, wireless providers, competitive local exchange carriers, and voice over internet procol (VOIP) services vying for customers. And the rise of broadband Internet access gives most Americans access to an unprecedented array of digital applications, communications services, and content.

The FCC in Jeopardy

In this environment, the foundations for the FCC's legal authority are unsteady. Most of the FCC's statutory mandate is tied to specific services and networks: over-the-air broadcasting, telecommunications, wireless communication, cable television, and satellite communications. Remarkably, the Communications Act, even after its 1996 revisions, makes virtually no reference to the internet. It includes a definition of "information services" (47 U.S.C. §153(20)), but no language whatsoever about the FCC's authority regarding such services. It was inevitable that this weakness at the foundation would ultimately destabilize the agency.

When broadband data services were a minor adjunct to the established communications industry, that statutory white space was an advantage. It allowed the FCC to keep nascent services such as VOIP and streaming online video away from regulatory obligations that might have quashed innovation (FCC, 1998). Starting in 2002, the FCC issued a series of decisions that defined broadband offerings, even those integrated with traditional telecommunications functions, as information services (FCC, 2002). It therefore placed them outside its specific regulatory mandates.

Today, broadband-based communications services are becoming the norm. The third largest residential phone company in the U.S. is Comcast (Comcast, 2013), running all its traffic over VOIP, and the two companies ahead of it – AT&T and Verizon – have plans to do the same (Troianovski, 2012; Baumgartner, 2013). Video and wireless voice services are also moving toward converged platforms based on the internet protocol. What happens when they get there?

Incumbent providers have a simple answer. AT&T is arguing that all major regulatory obligations disappear once its network is based on the IP (AT&T, 2013), and Verizon is claiming that its broadband internet service represents a form of speech immune from regulation under the First Amendment (Verizon & MetroPCS, 2013). Broadcasters and cable operators have for years been arguing that structural regulation of media is no longer required in the digital era. Even if these arguments fail, the damage has been done. Without a clear case for continued regulatory oversight, every significant FCC action may involve a pitched multi-year battle over fundamental questions, similar to what we've seen with the FCC's 2010 Open Internet order to promote network neutrality (FCC, 2010) and the efforts to update media ownership rules (*Prometheus Radio Project* v. *FCC*, 2011).

The Future of Cyberspace and Communications

Is there still a role for the FCC in an era of abundance? Yes. There are some problems that competition does not solve and general-purpose statutory frameworks do not address. The fact that there are now hundreds of channels on the television dial and millions of sites on the internet does not, in itself, mean that the informational and communicative needs of a healthy democracy are being met. Nor does the unifying force of digital convergence necessarily ensure the dynamic cycles of innovation and creative disruption, when networks are inherently subject to bottlenecks and structural advantages of incumbency or scale.

While a significant portion of the FCC's activity involves general-purpose economic regulation, an equally significant portion does not. Once it gets beyond the Open Internet proceeding, the FCC faces a set of issues that will define its twenty-first-century mission. These issues fall into three broad categories: non-economic considerations, interconnection, and vestigial scarcities. Each provides a justification for an agency with the mission and history of the FCC.

Non-Economic Considerations

The FCC has the expertise and bureaucratic scale to confront the exceedingly complex, fact-specific questions at the nexus of electronic media and the public interest. The fundamental question to be answered is whether a special-purpose entity of this type remains necessary. Why not address media and telecommunications industry concerns the same way concerns in the steel or retail industries are addressed: through general-purposes mechanisms such as the Federal Trade Commission, the antitrust arm of the Department of Justice, or common-law courts?

The fact of the matter is that while all these are valuable, none can play the necessary roles that the FCC occupies. Antitrust and consumer protection law are generally retrospective. They get involved to fix problems more than to prevent them. However, the beneficiaries of communications and media networks are not only the users and competitors of today; they include innovators and non-traditional producers whose output will never see the light of day without the kind of pro-active oversight the FCC can provide. To put it another way, the social value of infrastructure lies largely in spillover effects, which traditional economic levers often fail to recognize (Frischmann, 2012).

Or consider questions about cybersecurity and internet governance. These have become increasingly prominent in light of growing international cyber-attacks and revelations about surveillance by the National Security Agency. The FCC, as the expert civilian regulator of communications networks, is an important counterweight to the security community's push for ever-greater access to private data.

There are also some issues the FCC handles that are inescapably normative. For example, what level of broadband service should be available to all Americans, regardless of the cost of reaching certain rural areas? What constitutes excessive concentration of media ownership in a vibrant democracy? In a natural disaster, how long should wired phone networks operate after a power outage, and who will provide emergency information? These and other commitments go to the social contract inherent in public communications networks. The FCC will have to rethink how they can be maintained in a very different technical and competitive environment, but at least the FCC is positioned to ask those questions.

Interconnection

In a converged digital world, no provider can reach all customers with all services and content (Werbach, 2014). Every market participant must interconnect with others. However, interconnection allows for bottlenecks, even in a competitive market. Companies that control essential content or access to customers may act as *de facto* monopolists.

Notably, interconnection is relevant both to telecommunications and media. Telephone companies cannot refuse to interconnect with one another, and must do so on reasonable and non-discriminatory terms (47 U.S.C. §151(a),(c)). Internet providers have no such requirements. What happens, then, when those phone companies transition to IP technologies, and refuse to interconnect with Skype or Google Fiber? Or when Verizon provides insufficient network ports to terminate traffic from online content providers? (A situation that actually arose.) (See Engebretson, 2013.) The right answer isn't to extend all the pricing rules for telephone service to a very different environment, but neither is it to walk away from the reality that voluntary agreements don't always materialize.

The equivalent issue in the media world is retransmission consent. Under the 1992 Cable Act, broadcasters can demand payment for retransmitting their signals on cable and satellite systems (FCC, 2011). Increasingly, these have become high-stakes games of chicken, with broadcasters demanding increasing payments and other consideration for both their over-the-air and affiliated cable channels. In a number of cases, channels have been blocked for viewers in some cities, and the end result is spiraling programming costs passed on to cable and satellite subscribers (Yu, 2013).

In both of these cases, the FCC needs to forge a way forward that promotes commercially reasonable good faith negotiations, as opposed to the detailed price and content regulation it traditionally imposed. With over-the-top (OTT) video services such as Netflix becoming the largest source of internet traffic and growing powers in the media world, whether and how the FCC rises to this challenge will define the shape of the marketplace.

Vestigial Scarcities

Finally, even in a world of abundance, some things remain constrained. The FCC should focus its attention on those scarcities that endure.

One such scarcity is human attention. No matter how much media is theoretically available from how many sources, our brains can only focus on a limited set of information. In fact, the explosion of content sources exacerbates the difficulty of finding what we want in the profusion of choices. Thus, for example, where traditionally public media was seen as an infrastructure problem—for-profit broadcasters wouldn't provide enough, so non-profit channels had to be created—it is now increasingly a problem of search and aggregation (Goodman, 2004).

A second category of stubbornly persistent scarcities are those created by the legal system itself. In particular, the scarcity of wireless spectrum represents not a fundamental limit in capacity but artificial restrictions on access through the established pattern of licenses (Werbach, 2004). FCC action is necessary both to enable spectrum sharing and to reallocate frequencies from both private and governmental licensees who make inefficient use of them.

The FCC's 2010 National Broadband Plan proposed a goal, subsequently adopted by the Obama Administration, of freeing up 500 MHz of spectrum in ten years (Obama, 2010). The central initiative involved is the so-called incentive auction, which will compensate TV broadcasters for voluntarily relinquishing spectrum needed for wireless broadband. More recently, the President's Council of Advisors on Science and Technology (PCAST) Policy proposed an ambitious framework for a shared spectrum access regime (PCAST, 2012). Both of these will be technically and economically complex, multi-year initiatives that cannot proceed without the expertise the FCC brings to the table. And, without them, the wireless industry that is experiencing massive growth with the profusion of smartphones, tablets, wearables, and connected devices faces a calamitous spectrum crunch.

Conclusion

Preserving the FCC's legal authority will, inescapably, expand the scope of industries it touches. If Google provides a real-time voice communications service and Microsoft is a video services provider over cable networks, it makes no sense to exclude them from conversations at the FCC. Doing so would create a yawning opportunity for the traditional regulated companies, whom those new entrants happen to depend on, to free themselves from regulation through technical reconfiguration.

This is not to say that Apple should be subject to the exact same rules as Verizon or CBS. The FCC will have to develop appropriate distinctions to reflect real differences in the marketplace. The point is that if companies benefit from the open, interconnected, competitive network ecosystem that the FCC preserves, that comes with reciprocal obligations. This will likely be a painful battle, but ultimately one that creates a sounder footing for all the affected industries.

The FCC must evolve, but it should remain as relevant as ever in a converged digital world.

References

AT&T. (2013). Comments to Federal Communications Commission Report and Order and Further Notice of Proposed Rulemaking, Connect America Fund et al, FCC 11-161.

Baumgartner, J. (2013, July 22). Verizon FiOS rolls out 500-meg internet tier offers. *Multichannel News*. Retrieved from http://www.multichannel.com/distribution/verizon-fios-rolls-out-500-meg-internet-tier/144521

Comcast. (2013). Comcast reports 2nd quarter 2013 results. Retrieved from http://www.cmcsk.com/releasedetail.cfm?ReleaseID=781496

Engebretson, J. (2013, June 24). Verizon, Netflix dispute not just over peering; servers are new battlefield. *Telecompetitor*. Retrieved from http://www.telecompetitor.com/verizon-netflix-dispute-not-just-over-peering-servers-are-new-battlefield/

Federal Communications Commission [FCC]. (1998). Federal-state joint board on universal service, report to Congress. *F.C.C. Record*, 13, 531–532. Retrieved from http://www.fcc.gov/Bureaus/Common_Carrier/Reports/fcc98067.pdf

Federal Communications Commission [FCC]. (2002). Inquiry concerning high-speed access to the internet over cable & other facilities, declaratory ruling and notice of proposed rulemaking. *F.C.C. Record*, 17, 4839.

Federal Communications Commission [FCC]. (2010). Preserving the open internet; broadband industry practices, report and order. *FCC Record*, 25, 17905.

Federal Communications Commission [FCC]. (2011). Amendment of the Commission's rules related to retransmission consent, notice of proposed rulemaking. *FCC Record*, 26, 2718.

Frischmann, B. (2012). *Infrastructure: The social value of shared resources*. Oxford: Oxford University Press.

Goodman, E. (2004). media policy out of the box: Content abundance, attention scarcity, and the failures of digital markets. *Berkeley Technology Law Journal*, 19, 1389–1472.

Hazlett, T. (1990). The rationality of U.S. regulation of the broadcast spectrum. *Journal of Law and Economics*, 33, 133–175. doi:10.1086/467202

Nuechterlein, J., & Weiser, P. (2013). *Digital crossroads: American telecommunications policy in the internet age* (2nd ed.). Cambridge, MA: MIT Press.

Obama, B. (2010). Presidential memorandum, unleashing the wireless broadband revolution. Retrieved from http://www.whitehouse.gov/the-press-office/presidential-memorandum-unleashing-wireless-broadband-revolution

President's Council of Advisors on Science and Technology. (2012). Report to the President: Realizing the full potential of government-held spectrum to spur economic growth. Retrieved from http://www.whitehouse.gov/sites/default/files/microsites/ostp/pcast_spectrum_report_final_july_20_2012.pdf

Prometheus Radio Project v. FCC (2011). 652 F. 3d 431 (3rd Circuit).

Troianovski, A. (2012). AT&T move signals end of the copper-wire era. *Wall Street Journal*, November 12. Retrieved from http://online.wsj.com/news/articles/SB10001424127887324439804578104820999974556

Verizon & MetroPCS. (2013). *Verizon v. FCC*, D.C. Circuit Court of Appeals, No. 11-1355, Joint Brief. January 18.

Werbach, K. (2004). Supercommons: Toward a unified theory of wireless communication. *Texas Law Review*, 82, 863–973.

Werbach, K. (2014). No dialtone: The end of the public switched telephone network. *Federal Communications Law Journal*, 66, 1–60.

Yu, R. (2013, July 16). Race for TV broadcast fees raises questions: Consumers pick up the bill, and it's on the way up. *U.S.A Today*, July 16, p. 1B.

"What Is Wrong Cannot Be Made Right[1]"? Why Has Media Reform Been Sidelined in the Debate Over "Social Justice" in Israel?[2]

Amit Schejter & Noam Tirosh

When hundreds of thousands of Israelis took to the streets in the summer of 2011, protesting the high cost of living and demanding "social justice," the ills of the media system including its concentration, the growing digital divide, and the implosion of public broadcasting were not made part of the social movement's agenda. This study employs a justice-based theory for media, analyzing three types of "products" of the social movement: the unionization of media workers, the establishment of alternative media, and the reports recommending regulatory/institutional reform. We attempt to understand why media reform, an essential element without which social justice cannot be fully achieved, has been sidelined in the debate over the ways to achieve "social justice" in Israel.

Hundreds of thousands of Israelis took to the streets in the summer of 2011 to take part in an unprecedented protest calling for "social justice" (Filc & Ram, 2013; Wallach, 2012). Situated chronologically between the "Arab Spring" and the rise of the worldwide "Occupy" movements, which were both focused on a call for democracy and social justice and which were popularly associated with the presumed impact of "social media" on their emergence and sustenance, the Israeli social movement of 2011, too, was identified as a "Facebook revolution" (Landau, 2011).

The media play a central role in the functioning of democracies. Even in the minimal description of liberal democracy, free expression, is required for the democratic system to function in a meaningful way (Zakaria, 1997). Hence, the maintenance of a democratic regime is rooted in the maintenance of a free media system, and the media play a role in maintaining and developing democracy both formally and substantially. Contemporary digital media create the opportunity for a new type of mediated sociability. This opportunity emanates from the four characteristics that differentiate them from their electronic predecessors: they allow for an abundance of channels and content; they are accessible in both stationary and mobile forms; users can utilize them to meaningfully interact with each other; and personal communications can employ multimedia functions (Schejter & Tirosh, 2014a).

In the previous generation of electronic media, the concern for its appropriate functioning in support of democracy focused on overcoming the scarcity of opportunities for expression emanating from its technological capabilities. It was mostly a concern for freedom of the media. Identifying the unique characteristics of contemporary media creates an opportunity for policy seeking to ensure that it serves democracy and, to focus on a just distribution of its resources, beyond the conversation about freedom (Schejter & Tirosh, 2014b).

In this study, we sought to explore whether indeed a conversation about reforming the media was part of the debate about social justice in the 2011 Israeli social protest, especially since the movement was so strongly associated with, and apparently made much use of, media to advance its cause. We assumed that since the Israeli media structure had been suffering from distortions that made the distribution of its assets unequal, and since one of the battle cries of the protest movement focused on the relationship between capital, government, and the media ("*hon-shilton-itton*," which rhymes in Hebrew), media reform would be an issue the protest would focus on.

Social Justice and Media Reform

What is the role of contemporary media in twenty-first-century social movements? Most of these social movements refrained from demanding radical media reform, and they did not try to reshape the power relations that nourish the democratic deficit caused by the media (Hackett & Carroll, 2006). One can identify a gap between "conventional activism" and media activism as "[t]he former makes strategic use of the media (whether mainstream or its own) as a means toward some other political end; the latter approaches media as an (at least interim) end in itself" (p. 88). Indeed, Napoli (2007) asserts that "media reform is unique in that the alteration of media is both a means and ends for the movement" (p. 52), resulting in a tradition in which social movements "take for granted the existing structures and practices of the established media" (Hackett & Carroll, 2006, p. 45). Media reform aimed at media democratization is not compatible with this situation. Hackett and Carroll (2006) point out three different strategies of media reformers:

- an internal reform of the media field by the media workers;
- the establishment of "alternative media," creating "autonomous spaces in civil society"; and
- the attempt to effect change of state rules, regulations and policy.

But what is the relationship between media reform and social justice? The unique position of contemporary media renders it a forum that can potentially enable the participation of all, not limited to a closed community in which rules of seniority, aristocracy, and exclusivity may apply (Schejter & Yemini, 2007). "Consequently, it creates the need for rules that negate all forms of tyranny and oppression, whether initiated by government or by dominance through wealth" (Schejter & Yemini, 2007, p. 171). Such rules require a conceptual leap from the existing normative choices that govern media regulation and are rooted in a utilitarian paradigm arising from an antiquated view of media technology to a new normative paradigm that is based on the opportunity contemporary media create for the strengthening of a participatory democracy. Adopting this paradigm will create an opportunity for those least advantaged by communications to partake in the new media arena and will guarantee that all ideas receive the same opportunity to be heard.

The Social Protest of 2011

The protests of the summer of 2011 were like no other protest in Israel's history. The demonstration organizers claimed for the first time to represent a social class— self-described as "the middle class" – and not an identifiable pressure or interest group as in the past. A 25-year-old student, Daphni Leaf, whose rental lease had run out perched a tent in the center of Tel Aviv's Rothschild Boulevard on July 14, 2011. She then created a Facebook "event," inviting her friends to join her, which they did.

During the two months following the erection of the first tent, "tent cities" emerged all over the country; weekly demonstrations took place on Saturday nights both in Tel Aviv and in other cities; and in the evenings people gathered in parks and boulevards to talk about social justice. In addition, unprecedented online activity took place, focusing on the protest and its messages and serving as a means of communications among the protesters and their leadership.

This online activity, and in particular the fact that the protest was initiated at its infancy by the creation of a "Facebook" group, led the media to frame the protest as a "Facebook" protest (Lior, 2011; Telem, 2011). Leaf's "Facebook protest" came on the heels of the references to a previous successful social movement campaign to lower the price of cottage cheese only a few months earlier, which had also been termed a "Facebook protest" (see Levin, 2012 and Landau, 2011).

Research Questions and Methodology

Protests perceived as associated with social networking applications have the potential to breach the gap between conventional activism and media activism identified by Hackett and Carroll (2006). The use of media is endemic to their very being and can be seen as a fundamental element contributing to their success. Protesters aware of this connection will thus highlight issues such as: fears of media control by government and large corporations; the digital divide; and the decline of public media. We decided therefore to ask:

- Has media reform been presented as a goal in the social protest of 2011 and its aftermath?
- If so, how? And if not, why?

In order to answer these questions we decided to study the emergence of the three forms of media reform:

- We searched for internal professional organizations established after the protest.
- We looked for alternative media formed after the protest. To identify the alternative media, we used the web site associated with the protest movement, "J14," and the list it provided of all the initiatives that were derived from the protesters activities.[3] While the "protest movement" itself is an elusive term and while it did not have a democratically elected representation or a formal structure, "J14" was universally identified with the movement. No other source challenges this claim nor presents itself as the "face" of the protest.
- We identified three types of by-products of the social protest, which were designed in order to affect state rules. We then conducted a textual analysis of these sources and identified every instance in which media reform or any other type of reform that may affect the media and telecommunications industries was mentioned.
- The sources identified for the third part of the analysis were:
- Official reports: The Trajtenberg committee report and minutes of meetings:[4] On August 10, Prime Minister Benjamin Netanyahu appointed a committee headed by the economist Professor Manuel Trajtenberg to recommend ways to "alleviate the burden of living in Israel."[5]
- Alternative reports: The Spivak/Yonah report: The protesters, while partially cooperating with the Trajtenberg Committee, formed their own "alternative" committee headed by two professors of Ben-Gurion University of the Negev: Avia Spivak, an economist and former deputy governor of the Bank of Israel and Yossi Yonah who teaches and studies political and educational philosophy. The Spivak-Yonah report was published as a book in the summer of 2012 (Spivak & Yonah, 2012).
- The platforms of the parties participating in the January 2013 general elections: Early elections were called in Israel in 2012, and took place in January 2013. The proximity to the protest led us to believe that the platforms of the parties competing for seats in the Knesset will refer to social justice issues.

Findings

Professional Organizations

A new journalists' union that was formed after the protests had close to 2,000 members and was recognized as the official representative body of the media workers in 14 media outlets by the end of August 2013 (http://itonaim.org.il/). In 2013, workers of two of the large private mobile operators—Bezeq's subsidiary *Pelephone* and the largest operator *Cellcom*—as well as those of the cable operator *Hot* unionized much to the discontentment and disapproval of their owners. Indeed, the effect of this wave of unionization on the industry, as a reform strategy, is yet to be assessed.

Alternative Media

Virtually all the internet activities generated by the social protest used different formats of alternative media. In some cases, the websites or Facebook pages served the internal communications of the protest movement, such as the protest movement's "situation room" (https://www.facebook.com/j14live/info) and the protest movements' blogging platform (http://k1789.org/?p=2646), which closed down in December 2012. In other cases, they served to raise awareness of the social protest by providing activists and the general public with alternative information: The "civil press" site had multiple u-stream (video) channels operated by activists across the country (civilpress.tv/)[6]; the "Israel Independent Press" (https://www.facebook.com/IsraelIndependentPress) is an English language resource about protest activities; and "Radio Beit Ha'am" broadcasts weekly alternative audio news and music (http://j14.org.il/j14live/beithaamradio). J14 listed on its web page also http://megafon-news.co.il/, which was indeed launched post the protest, but self describes itself as an independent unaffiliated cooperative of journalists.

The protest movement made institutional information available. Specifically, two initiatives launched in 2012 are "politiwatch" (http://www.politiwatch.co.il), which focuses on statements politicians make and checks their truthfulness, and "sand" (http://www.sandtalks.co.il), which in addition to rating the truthfulness of political talk also rates politicians based on their truthfulness. "J14" also mentioned the "open Knesset" initiative (http://oknesset.org) as related to the movement, though it was launched in 2009. It is a web-engine that allows users to follow the work of the Knesset and its members.

The other websites which the protest movement mentions are left-wing media sites, which existed long before the movement: http://www.haokets.org.il and http://www.tv.social.org.il. "J14," which had been kept updated since its launch, was folded in August 2013.

Structural Reform

The Trajtenberg Report

The Trajtenberg Committee, appointed by the Israeli government in response to the protest, was to present recommendations in five areas: changes to the government's priorities in order to alleviate the economic burden of the citizenry; changes in the mix of taxes; expansion of access to social services; enhancement of competition and efficiency in product and service markets in order to lower prices; and drawing of the implementation steps needed to advance the government's housing policy announced in July of 2011.

Concept of "justice"

The Trajtenberg report identifies three reasons for the social movement: economic hardship, injustice, and a general feeling of alienation (The Trajtenberg Report, Committee on Social Economic Change, 2011, p. 25). While not expanding on what "justice" means, the committee states that "the feeling of alienation emanates from the narrowing of the public-political discourse sphere in recent years and from the fact that the economic-social discourse has eroded and narrowed immensely" (The Trajtenberg report) The report, however, fails to make a connection between this phenomenon and the state of the media.

Public Participation

The committee adopted the Western narrative of "technological utopianism," stating that

> [T]here is no doubt that technology made a vital contribution to [the rise in public participation]. The Internet and cellular communications allow a direct and immediate connection from everyone to everyone else and the social networks allow multi-participant interactions not limited by time or by space. This way the few with initiative can jump start powerful processes that extend over vast publics and no central governmental body can stop, navigate or prevent this. (Trajtenberg Report, p. 54)

Public participation, thus, was mentioned in the report itself in enthusiastic terms, but with no concrete policy recommendations. With regards to its own work, the committee stated that it has "identified from the start the importance of maintaining a wide range of channels that would allow it to maintain contact with the public" (p. 249). It also stated that "the participation processes that were developed and utilized by the committee were influenced by international trends ... of a gradual transition from a representative democracy to a participatory/deliberative democracy" (p. 253) and that technological advances allowing a wide range of inclusive channels were effective and very helpful to the committee's effort in this regard. In its recommendations regarding the "principles of the social and economic policy" the committee report states that the government should adopt a model of "participatory democracy" when planning changes in policy that affect the public, but with no details. Such participation, states the report, strengthens democracy and helps balance the public interest with those of "powerful economic players" (p. 37; article 10). "The new Israelis," it adds,

> [D]emand that their voices are heard, not as a one-time act during a demonstration, but in a structured and routine manner in the new "agora." This is an announcement regarding the creation of a participatory democracy, lively, demanding and brave, which is very different from the patterns we have been acquainted with so far. (p. 53)

The Trajtenberg Committee tried to overcome the inherent suspicion in governmental committees trying to cope with political unrest by stating in the committee's letter of appointment that "during its work, the committee will hold a dialogue with different sectors within the Israeli public, including representatives of groups and organizations, and will listen to their ideas and positions with regards to possible policy steps in the different areas." The notion of openness was critical for the success of the committee's work, whether it was intended to be a public relations ploy or whether the government truly intended to engage in adopting significant reforms that would restructure the economy. Professor Trajtenberg met with protesters in the "tent cities" they erected in the center of Tel Aviv (Malka & Zayton, 2011), and a special team working for the committee and known as "Team Manuel" (http://www.teammanuel2011.org.il/) was charged with communicating over social web applications (Datel, 2013).

The minutes of the committee meetings reveal that Team Manuel was at least as interested in providing public relations to the committee and its chair as it was to actually creating a dialogue with the public. On the committee's sixth meeting, on September 13, 2011, the head of the team states that:

> We are looking at four stages in our work [...] build[ing] credibility [...] It worked very well [...] After that we reached the stage of public inclusion [...] surfers on the Internet were very excited by it, the numbers speak for themselves, [...] [But] now we've reached the tough stage, the somewhat sleepy stage, that because the committee works behind closed doors it is very hard on the surfers and it is important you should know that the people want information.

Indeed, committee members were also aware of this double-edged effort—PR on the one hand and dialogue with the public on the other—and reference to both is made in the minutes. It is incumbent to remember, however, that the minutes themselves were kept under wraps for eighteen months until a court order made them public. This alone suggests that "public participation" and the use of contemporary media to enhance it may have been genuine on behalf of the committee but not necessarily on the government's agenda. The Director General of the National Insurance Institute (roughly the equivalent of Social Security in the US), a committee member, stated at the August 16 meeting that "we have to invest in all the developed technological apparatuses to give the feeling that [we are] connected, talking, understanding, listening." Committee members also made the distinction between "public participation" and "public input." "These are two separate things," said the Accountant General, a committee member, at the September 6 meeting,

> [W]hen we say public inclusion it means that in every place in which decisions are made sits someone from the public within the decision making, and I just want to say that in my public capacity we take the public interest into consideration and slowly do things that are good for the public.

In the August 16 meeting the Accountant General stated that

> [T]here is always an advantage for decision makers in a certain distance from the public [...] a committee is sitting here, it has collective wisdom [...] why do I say this? Because let's not exaggerate, we are living among the people, we are not some disconnected people. We are all with small government salaries, we [also] need to fund the [rise in] the cost of living.

Digital Divide

Committee members were also not blind to the fact that there was a digital divide in Israeli society, and that the divide had an effect on the ability of the public to partake in the conversation. The Accountant General stated at the August 16 meeting that

> [T]he center of our activity is not against the tent-dwellers but rather against the public consciousness that supports them. When you utilize a tool such as the Internet it is not a tool for the lower decile in Be'er Sheva,[7] it is a tool for the upper decile.

At the September 13 meeting she added that "We always remind ourselves that sitting in front of these media are usually the stronger in society [...] because if they have access and accessibility, they are young and they are educated." However, these are the only references made to the digital divide in the meeting minutes. No mention of the divide is made in the committee's report, and no policies to overcome it were suggested.

Media and Telecommunication Reform

The media are mentioned in a limited number of contexts in the report, always as a means, never as a goal in themselves. Article 9 of the recommendations sees the media as a form for bettering the government's work in providing services to, and communicating with, the citizenry (The Trajtenberg Report, pp. 48–4). Specifically the report recommends using information and communication technologies (ICTs) to strengthen the enforcement capabilities of the tax authorities, in order to limit the "friction between the tax authorities and the public" (The Trajtenberg Report, p. 95) The result of this recommendation was the launching of "the whistleblower," a tool for citizens to call anonymously and squeal on their friends and acquaintances who are cheating the tax system. It also recommends creating information services for those using public transportation (The Trajtenberg Report, p. 148), digitizing (or rather uploading portable documents of) school books and allowing citizens to use computer communications to import goods from abroad whose value does not exceed $300 without the need to pay taxes on them. Access to ICTs is not mentioned as a goal in itself or as a means for democratization or the achievement of social justice. In a single mention (The Trajtenberg Report, p. 126), the report states that the ultra-orthodox community is not equipped to join the workforce lacking basic computer skills. The recommendation, therefore, is to add "computers" as a basic study in the ultra-orthodox school system (The Trajtenberg Report, p. 39).

In its only reference to media as a public good, the committee sees "public service media" as anachronistic. "If in the past," states the report, "communications were a government service like any other service, it is an anachronism today and in most countries in the world these services have long been privatized and lively markets of advanced and diverse communications exist" (The Trajtenberg Report, p. 41). Within its framing of communications as a consumer service, the report recommends lowering the taxation on "entertainment and electronic products" and on "mobile phones," both in the context of the introduction of further competition in the mobile phone market by the government, which was to begin within a year of the report's publication (The Trajtenberg Report, p. 176). Indeed the committee's mandate was limited, and the media were not specified as part of the committee's agenda, but the committee could have chosen to discuss media and telecommunications reform as they can fall under "access to social services" through combating the digital divide for example, or through promoting "public media" as an alternative to the existing commercially dominated sphere, through reference to the concentration of the media market as contributor to high advertising prices, or in itself as a market in which prices are high. It chose not to.

Spivak/Yonah Report

The Spivak/Yonah report (Spivak & Yonah, 2012), which was initiated by a group of academics and social activists supporting the social protest was in fact an amalgamation of a number of reports on different topics. The topics addressed were housing, transportation, land, planning, health, welfare, employment, and education. In addition, the report dealt with the more generalized issues: public administration, law and "deliberative democracy." Media and telecommunications issues, if mentioned, are sporadically dispersed in the different chapters. Thus for example, the constitutional framework the committee focusing on "law" recommended introducing a "social bill of rights," which includes the basic rights for an honorable life, equality, access to natural resources, a government reporting obligation, housing, health, education, social welfare, employment, unionizing and worker rights. It refrains from mentioning access to broadband (or even to information), an issue that had started making its way to progressive constitutions worldwide in recent years.[8] When it comes to media and telecommunications, the Spivak/Yonah report was not much different from the government's sanctioned report although it briefly mentions some media and telecommunications issues in the context of "Israel as a welfare state" and "lowering prices."

Concept of Justice

The Spivak/Yonah report criticizes what it perceives as the Trajtenberg report's "justice concept." "Their justice concept," claim Spivak and Yonah, "does not recognize the basic social rights of an individual" (2012, p. 31). These, in their eyes include the government creating a safety net for the citizenry in the fields of health, education, welfare, affordable housing, and fair employment (p. 33). The protest, claim the authors, reflected the protesters' demand to allow the public to influence the decision-making processes at the power centers of Israeli politics (p. 40). In addition, they state that the values in which the authors of the different reports based their recommendations included: equal opportunity, closing of gaps, distributive justice, mutual solidarity, and deliberative democracy (pp. 33–34).

Public Participation

The Spivak/Yonah report supports a new model of deliberative democracy. It is somewhat more skeptical than the Trajtenberg report with regards to the advancement made so far in this direction and states that "this move is in its beginning and its success so far has been limited" (p. 43). While the Trajtenberg report describes deliberative democracy as something that is "emerging," the Spivak/Yonah report describes it as an ideal form of governing. Yet, while the Trajtenberg report makes a connection (weak as it may be) between technology and participation, Spivak/Yonah fails to do so.

Media and Telecommunication Reform

Similar to the Trajtenberg report, the alternative report also sees computer communications as a means for providing government services more efficiently and recommends initiating "an operative plan for the improvement of service to the citizen by instilling quality methods, client satisfaction polls, decentralized service and information through the Internet" (Spivak & Yonah, 2012, p. 85) in the chapter on "public administration." There is no parallel mention in the Spivak/Yonah report though of the random list of "services" (digital books, information services for public transportation and for the importation of goods) the Trajtenberg report proposes. While the Trajtenberg report proposed introducing "computers" to the *Haredi* education system, the Spivak/Yonah report mentions in the context of "education" the need for "learning and computer communication spheres" (p. 349). It also proposes in the chapter dealing with employment, "raising consciousness for workers' rights" through advertising "in the relevant media for the populations suffering the most from violation of their rights, such as populations for which Hebrew is not their main language" (p. 309). The fact that there may be less access to ICTs among these very populations is discussed elsewhere, and the alternative report recommends strengthening the capability of citizens to take part in the development of policy. The report states in the context of welfare that "for this [cause] the availability and connectivity of people to internet networks [is important]—in particular the poor who suffer technological exclusion" (p. 280). One more mention of the media industries appears in the sub-chapter on "lowering monopolistic profit and lowering prices" in the "economy" report, in which the report states that "out of concern to the freedom of the press and the electronic media, the holdings of large media by owners of large businesses in other sectors of the economy, should be prohibited" (p. 114). Indeed, even for the protesters' "alternative" agenda, the media and their concentration, while a "freedom of the press" issue are framed in an economic frame.

Party Platforms[9]

While the early elections that took place in January of 2013 were not necessarily a direct result of the social protest of 2011 they were perceived as associated with them. Many of the parties vying for votes focused on a "social" rather than on a "political" agenda—which in Israel is synonymous with the relations with the Arab world and the Palestinians in particular—an uncommon phenomena in the Israeli political culture.

The largest party in both the outgoing and incoming Knesset was the *Likud*. The *Likud*, which competed in 2013 in an alignment with the *Israel Beiteinu* party, chose not to publish a platform at all (Karni, 2012). While such a move is rare, probably unprecedented in the 40-year history of the *Likud* and the 65-year history of ruling parties in Israel, the *Likud*'s advertising was attentive to the mood of the social protest and combined "social" and "political" messages. At the height of the campaign, the *Likud* introduced a series of billboard ads, each listing an "achievement" of the outgoing government and a check mark next to it (Wolf, 2013). Among these, social issues took a front row. Particularly noticeable was the ad promoting one of the most popular economic reforms of the outgoing government—licensing new mobile operators, a move which resulted in a dramatic drop in mobile phone service prices. Hence within the *Likud*'s platform, communication reform framed the citizenry as consumers.

The newly formed populist party *Yesh Atid* ("There is a Future") achieved a surprising second place showing in the elections. *Yesh Atid* published a very detailed platform, however media reform was not mentioned. References to the media appeared in the context of reforms in other sectors of the government's activity—small business licensing, foreign policy and sports regulation.

The Labor party, which ended as the third largest in the elections, and which espouses a social-democrat agenda, used a dialogue over the internet with party members to develop the party's platform. However, media reform was not mentioned in the party's platform, and the only reference to the media is by stating that new immigrants have established and consume media in their own languages, which is a problem, as it may testify to the fact that a substantial part of the immigrants do not see in Israel a place in which they feel secure.

Only the fourth largest party, the religious *Bayit Yehudi* ("Jewish Home") had a proactive media agenda promising to

> [W]ork towards the goal of making media in Israel more balanced. Not through legislation, but by uncovering reality. Today most senior media professionals in the

state are on the left edge of the political map. This is a distorted situation that hurts freedom of expression in the country.

The Democratic Front for Peace and Equality (of which the Communist party is the central faction) reads the media content somewhat differently. "The incitement against the Arab citizens of the state, which is delivered by official spokespersons and which is prevalent in parts of the educational and media systems," it states, "inflames a racist atmosphere." The party thus believes that

> in order for Israel to be democratic, tolerant and just, the media of mass communications need to integrate in the diffusion of different cultures and in the battle against ethnic discrimination.

"The Movement," a faction of the former *Kadima* party, a centrist coalition founded by the late prime minister Ariel Sharon, mentioned in its platform the limited access to resources that are controlled by a small interest group, invoking the maxim popularized by the protest movement "capital-government-media" (which, as mentioned above, rhymes in Hebrew). In the operative part of the platform, however, the only mention of communications is with regards to a proposal to open an online bank to infuse more competition in the banking market. Similarly *Meretz*, a Zionist-left wing party, calls for a battle against concentration in markets in general and mentions the need to set regulatory constraints on a few of them, specifically mentioning "the communications sector." *Meretz* also decries the fact that the rise in public debt leads to collection procedures taken against individuals, 61 Pct. of which are won by powerful players: the government, banks and communication corporations (probably referring to mobile phone and multichannel television operators).

Discussion

The social justice movement in Israel peaked in the summer of 2011 and indeed the media, new and old, were an important tool serving the movement's organization. Services monitoring the web estimated that in the first few months of 2011 more than 2,000 protest groups were created over social applications (Globes, 2011). At the same time, the protesters tuned in to traditional media: the main source of news for 56% of the protesters, according to a non-representative poll of 142 "tent dwellers" on Rothschild Boulevard, were the traditional media and only for 35% were they social networking applications, such as Twitter and Facebook (Hetsroni & Lowenstein, 2012).

However, the precursor to the summer 2011 events, known as the "cottage revolution" (a result of which cottage cheese prices dropped some 40%) demonstrated that while social networking applications can serve to generate support for a cause, the transition from support to action and influence is still in the hands of the traditional media (even if it is on the web) and that the protesters need to tailor their messages to this "media logic" (Levin, 2012). When the protest movement was attempting to re-emerge in the summer of 2012, its voice was muted by traditional media, which—all at once—covered it as an insignificant event, framed it in negative terms, and framed stories of a social nature as separate from the protest (Iram, 2012). The amount of reporting on the protests dropped in June 2012 by 40% in comparison to the previous year (Grunzweig, 2012). Indeed, as much as the media were responsible for raising the visibility of the protest in its infancy, they contributed to its demise (Iram, 2012, p. 27). Yet the call for media reform and even a call for access reform were clearly absent from the conversation. Why did that happen? How could that have happened? We would like to speculate and offer three plausible explanations for this phenomenon:

1. Seeing "alternative media" as a platform for change

Establishing alternative media can be seen as a type of media reform strategy (Hackett & Carroll, 2006), and indeed alternative media challenge the basic structure of traditional media by their mere existence (Atton, 2008). This logic could very well be behind the disregard for media reform as a required element in any kind of social reform by the protesters' movement, which was invested in establishing alternative media outlets. Studies have demonstrated that media activists trying to promote change by working from "within" the media are less likely to voluntarily critique the ills of the media structure (Hackett & Adam, 1999). However, the assumption that alternative media alone can promote change does not really hold water for long, and there are a variety of reasons for this: first, audiences are still attentive to the traditional media (Averbuch, 2012), and there is no online outlet that can compete in its popularity with commercial radio or television. Second, the established media are the dominant players in the new media world. Adding marginal voices alongside them cannot effect any significant change in public opinion or social reality. Third, without an established financial backbone the "alternatives" generally fold. They need a powerful organization to back them or a structure that sustains them. The closing down of J14 itself, which was attributed to internal disputes between the leaders of the movement (Mizbala, 2013) is probably the best evidence to the futility of the "alternative media approach."

2. The neo-liberal takeover of the discourse

The neo-liberal discourse that swept the policy-making debate in general and the communications policy debate in particular has been able to eliminate any discussion of media as a public good and has left them to be regarded as commercial entities. The Trajtenberg committee focused on only a small sample of web services when discussing the role of media in the social change platform they were to design. All the examples were of a consumer nature and none were designed to back the hyped-up "participatory democracy" discourse with any concrete plan or with a "social media" plan in particular.

Surprisingly, the Spivak/Yonah report buys into the same jargon. Public broadcasting, for example, is mentioned in a long list of services that need reform, the media market is not seen as one requiring intervention, and the digital divide is absent from the conversation.

The protest movement of 2011 spoke a new civic language that connected groups that were otherwise unable to communicate with each other: Jews and Arabs, "old-timers" and immigrants (Wallach, 2012). For a brief moment, members of distinct publics advocated for reforms that were to benefit other social classes (Rosenhak & Shalev, 2012), and the "neoliberal economy and its unbearable social repercussions" (Alimy, 2012) became the bon ton. Yet, when the reform "committees" were assembled, they were dominated by economists, and "economic speak" dominated their discussions, and subsequently their recommendations (Paz-Fuchs, 2011). Within the "economic speak" the media are functioning properly: they behave as a commercial market and as such they do not require to be reformed.

In addition, media attention was first turned away from the protest following a terrorist attack along the southern border and "the chilling effect of the patriotic, state-loyalist discourses which reached unprecedented prominence in Israeli society silenced and subdued the debate" (Gordon, 2012, p. 350). Even on alternative media, critics see this transition of attention as normal and acceptable, stating that the media cannot focus on two parallel and purportedly disconnected narratives at the same time (e.g. Dror, 2011; Mor, 2013).

3. The protest movement as a "blinded" middle class and "Facebook protest"

As mentioned, the protesters were not cut along the traditional lines of social gaps to the extent that they were seen as creating a new "subjective collective" (Filc & Ram, 2013). However, this new "class" consisted mostly of the more educated and less-affluent component of the middle class (Filc & Ram, 2013). The social protest has thus not been a movement of the proletariat seeking social justice or of the poor. The protesters were well connected to the internet and the "digital divide" was not an issue to be troubled with. The lack of access to the media is not only something they do not see as a problem in part because the protesters are largely a middle-class that was created by the information economy and who expect access to the media as a given. A further contributing factor to this view of social reality is that the traditional media, as described above, attributed to social media applications the actual "power" of the protest. Feeling powerful negated any desire to call for change.

Conclusion

What generalizations, if any, can the short-lived social movement that emerged in Israel in 2011, and for whom communicative justice was apparently not a goal, provide to the media research community and to the media reform movement? The findings show that while a new professional organization for journalists was formed and while a plethora of alternative media outlets sprung out of the movement, the "Facebook protests" could not see beyond neo-liberal and commercial interests when discussing media reform and the protesters were blind to the need for structural institutional regulatory reform that may contribute to a communicatively just society.

Only three years later, the protests demonstrate that not only was there no change in the structure of Israeli media, but there was no real change in Israeli society with regards to the issues that were at the center of the protest: housing prices are still on the rise, social gaps are still growing, and government policy is not focused on social issues. In 2012, Israeli police summoned the activists of the 2011 protest and questioned them as to their future protest plans (Lior & Kobovitz, 2012), thus raising the fear that the goal of these interrogations was to chill and silence any future protest activities. Only a direct order from the Minister of Internal Security halted this practice. By 2014 the police crackdown on freedom of expression raised so much public alarm that the Ministry of Justice was forced to propose an amendment to the law that would scrap the police from the authority to indict protesters (Hoval, 2014).

The absence of social reform on the one hand and the assault on freedom of expression on the other raise the question whether introducing media reform to the social protest's agenda would not have made a difference in the chances of the protesters to succeed in maintaining their agenda within the public sphere.

The new form contemporary media take requires a different approach to media regulation in order to achieve social justice. Blinded by the neo-liberal takeover of public discourse, by its own middle-class wealth, by the constant use of contemporary media that makes its structure transparent, and by the instinctive acceptance of the existing security dominated talk, a social movement whose creation was so strongly associated and supported by an understanding of contemporary media's inner working and infrastructure missed a historic opportunity to demand a reform in access to it and in its control. If there was one lesson for this movement, after the dust has settled and virtually no reforms of any kind had taken place it is that social justice cannot be reached without a justice-based reform in the media.

Notes

[1]   Ecclesiastes 1:15.
[2]   This study has been supported by a Career Integration Grant awarded by the Marie Curie FP7 program of the European Union and by the I-CORE Program of the Planning and Budgeting Committee and the Israel Science Foundation (grant no. 1716/12). Both authors contributed equally to this study.
[3]   The site (http://j14.org.il/polimap/) does not exist anymore.
[4]   The minutes of the internal debates of the committee were sealed until the Supreme Court forced the government to uncover them in March 2013.
[5]   The committee's letter of appointment can be accessed at: http://hidavrut.gov.il/content/4244
[6]   The site does not exist anymore.
[7]   A stereotypically low-income city.
[8]   In such countries as Estonia (Woodward, 2003) Finland (Riesinger, 2009); France (*London Times*, *2009*); Greece (Constitution of Greece, 2009); and Spain (Reuters, 2009).
[9]   All party platforms were accessed online during the elections and are on file with authors.

References

Alimy, E. (2012). "Occupy Israel": A tale of startling success and hopeful failure. *Social Movement Studies: Journal of Social, Cultural and Political Protest, 11*, 402–407.

Atton, C. (2008). Alternative media theory and journalism practice. In M. Boler (Ed.) *Digital media and democracy: Tactics in hard times* (pp. 213–228). Cambridge, MA: MIT Press.

Averbuch, L. (2012, 19 June). Glued to the screen: Israelis watch television almost 4 hours a day. Retrieved from http://www.globes.co.il/news/article.aspx?did=1000758417 [in Hebrew].

Committee on Social Economic Change. (2011). *Toward the design of a more just Israeli society* (The Trajtenberg Report). Retrieved from http://hidavrut.gov.il/sites/default/files/%20%D7%9B%D7%9C%D7%9C%D7%99%D7%AA.pdf) [in Hebrew].

Constitution of Greece. (2009). Article 5A(2). Retrieved from http://www.hellenicparliament.gr/UserFiles/f3c70a23-7696-49db-9148-f24dce6a27c8/001-156%20aggliko.pdf

Datel, L. (2013, 24 February). Trachtenberg: "I am astonished at the ignorance in economics of the intelligent public." Retrieved from http://www.themarker.com/news/1.1936854 [in Hebrew].

Dror, Y. (August 21, 2011). Tweet me a new agenda. The 7th eye. Retrieved from http://www.the7eye.org.il/13705) [in Hebrew].

Filc, D., & Ram, U. (2013). Daphni Leaf's July 14th: The rise and fall of the social protest. *Theory and Critique, 41*, 17–43 [in Hebrew].

Globes. (2011, 4 August). The social protest in numbers: 2000 Facebook groups. Retrieved from http://www.globes.co.il/news/article.aspx?did=1000670717 [in Hebrew].

Gordon, U. (2012). Israel's 'tent protests': The chilling effect of nationalism. *Social Movement Studies: Journal of Social, Cultural and Political Protest, 11*, 349–355.

Grunzweig, E. (2012, 28 June). Study: Scope of reporting on social protest down 40 percent. Retrieved from http://www.haaretz.co.il/gallery/media/1.1742337 [in Hebrew].

Hackett, R., & Adam, M. (1999). Is media democratization a social movement? *Peace Review, 11*, 125–131.

Hackett, R., & Carroll, W. (2006). *Remaking media: The struggle to democratize public communication.* New York, NY: Routledge.

Hetsroni, A., & Lowenstein, H. (2012). Old or new? The media chosen by the Israeli "tent protest" movement. *Kesher, 43*, 13–22.

Hoval, R. (August 13, 2014). Ministry of Justice: The authority to indict protesters will be taken away from the police. Retrieved from http://www.haaretz.co.il/news/law/.premium-1.2405282 [in Hebrew].

Iram, S. (2012). *"The protest is back – (only) thousands showed up": Covering of the social protest in the Israeli press.* Jerusalem: Keshev —The Center for the Protection of Democracy in Israel [in Hebrew].

Karni, Y. (December 13, 2012). Couldn't be found: A journey in search of the Likud platform. Ynet. Retrieved from http://ynet.co.il.d4p.net/articles/0,7340,L-4319455,00.html [in Hebrew].

Landau, G. (8 August, 2011). "The Facebook effect"—Mark Zuckerberg is the one that enabled the tent protest. Retrieved from http://e.walla.co.il/?w=/266/1848103 [in Hebrew].

Levin, D. (2012). The cottage cheese boycott: "Internet logic" meets "media logic". *Kesher, 43*, 23–28 [in Hebrew].

Lior, I. (2011, 12 July). "The Facebook protest that will turn Habimah Square in Tel Aviv to a tent city." Retrieved from http://www.haaretz.co.il/news/education/1.1180154 [in Hebrew].

Lior, I., & Kobovitz, Y. (2012, 12 June). Social protest activists summoned for interrogation regarding their plans for the upcoming summer. Retrieved from http://www.haaretz.co.il/news/education/1.1729204 [in Hebrew].

London Times. (2009, June 12). Top French court declares internet access "basic human right". Retrieved from http://www.foxnews.com/story/2009/06/12/top-french-court-declares-internet-access-basic-human-right/

Malka, Y., & Zayton, Y. (2011, 15 August). Trajtenberg at the encampment: "You will design the future." Retrieved from http://www.ynet.co.il/articles/0,7340,L-4108844,00.html. [in Hebrew].

Mizbala (2013, 21 July) Hostile takeover? The social protest J14 has lost control over the protest site and the official Facebook page (mizbala.com/?p=74199).

Mor, G. (May 7, 2013). It's time to take ownership of the media. Holes in the net. Retrieved from http://www.holesinthenet.co.il/holesinthenet-media-story-1630) [in Hebrew].

Napoli, P. (2007). Public interest media activism and advocacy as a social movement: A review of the literature. McGannon Center Working Paper Series. Paper 21. Retrieved from http://fordham.bepress.com/mcgannon_working_papers/21

Paz-Fuchs, A. (2011). Justice under protest: Lawyers and the social protest of 2011. *Ma'asey Mishpat, 4*, 93–108.

Reuters (2009, November 17). Spain govt to guarantee legal right to broadband. Retrieved from http://www.reuters.com/article/2009/11/17/spain-telecoms-idUSLH61554320091117

Riesinger, D. (2009, October 14). Finland makes 1Mb broadband access a legal right. CNET. Retrieved from http://news.cnet.com/8301-17939_109-10374831-2.html

Rosenhak, Z., & Shalev, M. (2012). Distributive grievances and socio-political blockages: The role of middle-class youth in the Israeli social protest movement. Paper presented at the Social Justice and Democratization Conference. Buenos Aires. Argentina.

Schejter, A., & Yemini, M. (2007) "Justice, and only justice, you shall pursue": Network neutrality, the First Amendment and John Rawls' Theory of Justice. *Michigan Telecommunications and Technology Law Review, 14*, 137–174.

Schejter, A., & Tirosh, N. (2014a). New media policy: The redistribution of voice. In Y. Liu & R. Picard (Eds.), *Policy and marketing strategies for digital media* (pp. 73–86). London: Routledge.

Schejter, A., & Tirosh, N. (2014b). Social justice as an organizing principle for contemporary media policy. A paper presented at TPRC 42, The Research Conference on Communication, Information and Internet Policy. Arlington, VA, USA

Spivak, A., & Yonah, Y. (2012). *To do things different: A model for a well-ordered society.* Tel Aviv: Hakibutz Hameuchad [in Hebrew].

Telem, Y. (2011, 13 July). The Facebook protest goes to the street. *Yedioth Ahronoth.* Retrieved from http://article.yedioth.co.il/default.aspx?articleid=5114 [in Hebrew].

Wallach, Y. (2012). The politics of non-iconic space: Sushi, shisha, and a civic promise in the 2011 summer protests in Israel. *European Urban and Regional Studies, 20*, 150–154.

Wolf, P. (2013, January 2). Likud's campaign: No platform yet, new billboards yes. Walla! Retrieved from http://news.walla.co.il/elections/?w=/2780/2606138 [in Hebrew].

Woodward, C. (2003, July 1) Estonia, where being wired is a human right. *Christian Science Monitor.* Retrieved from http://www.csmonitor.com/2003/0701/p07s01-woeu.html

Zakaria, F. (1997). The rise of illiberal democracy. *Foreign Affairs, 76*(6), 22–43.

Index

Note: Page numbers followed by 'n' refer to notes